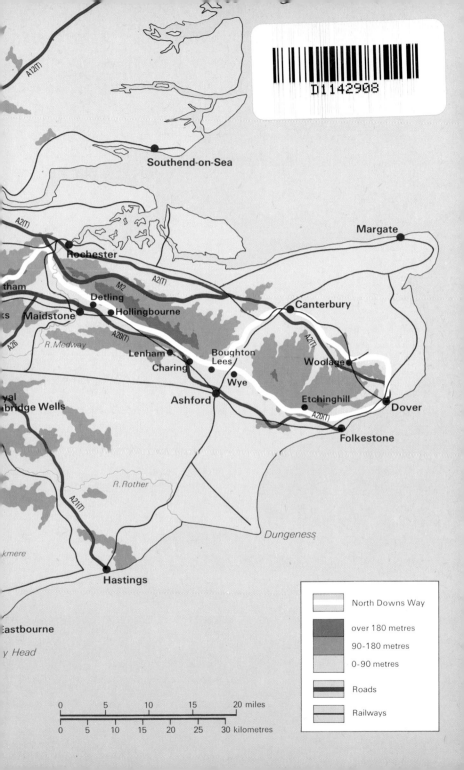

Key to cover illustration: 1 yew, 2 ash, 3 hogweed, 4 wayfaring-tree, 5 nettle-leaved bellflower, 6 poppies, 7 roebuck, 8 brimstone butterfly, 9 nightingale, 10 cuckoo, 11 yellowhammer, 12 carrion crow

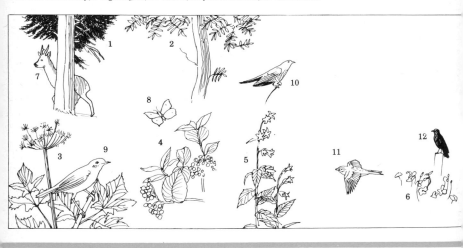

The North Downs Way

Denis Herbstein

Long-Distance Footpath Guide No 11

London: Her Majesty's Stationery Office 1982

Published for the Countryside Commission

Cover based on view near Trottiscliffe

The maps in this guide are extracts from Ordnance Survey 1:25,000 maps sheet nos. SU 84/94, TQ 04/14, 15, 24, 25/35, 45/55, 65/75, 66/76, 85/95, 86/96, 94, TR 04, 05/15, 13, 14, 23, 24/34, 25.

Drawings: Louis Mackay

Photographs: Archie Miles

Long-distance footpath guides published for the Countryside Commission by HMSO:

The Pennine Way, by Tom Stephenson: 120 pages, £3.95 net
The Cleveland Way, by Alan Falconer: 144 pages, £3.95 net
The Pembrokeshire Coast Path, by John H Barrett: 124 pages, £3.95 net.
Offa's Dyke Path, by John B Jones: 124 pages, £3.95 net
Cornwall Coast Path, by Edward C Pyatt: 120 pages, £3.95 net
The Ridgeway Path, by Seán Jennett: 120 pages, £3.95 net
South Downs Way, by Seán Jennett: 122 pages, £3.95 net
Dorset Coast Path, by Brian Jackman: 122 pages, £3.95 net
South Devon Coast Path, by Brian Le Messurier: 122 pages, £3.95 net
Somerset and North Devon Coast Path, by Clive Gunnell: 112 pages, £3.95 net

In preparation
Wolds Way

Government Bookshops:
49 High Holborn, London WC1V 6HB
13a Castle Street, Edinburgh EH2 3AR
41 The Hayes, Cardiff CF1 1JW
Brazennose Street, Manchester M60 8AS
Southey House, Wine Street, Bristol BS1 2BQ
258 Broad Street, Birmingham B1 2HE
80 Chichester Street, Belfast BT1 4JY

Government publications are also available through booksellers

Prepared for the Countryside Commission by the Central Office of Information.

Countryside Commission, John Dower House, Crescent Place, Cheltenham, Glos. GL50 3RA

The waymark sign is used in plaque or stencil form by the Countryside Commission on long-distance footpaths.

Printed in England for Her Majesty's Stationery Office by Linneys of Mansfield

ISBN 0 11 700905 9   Dd 696394   Pro 14955   C 300

Contents

Maps reference

ROADS AND PATHS

Not necessarily rights of way
M I or A 6(M)

M I or A 6(M)	Motorway
A 31(T)	Trunk road
A 35	Main road
B 3074	Secondary road
A 35	Dual carriageway
	Road generally more than 4m wide
	Road generally less than 4m wide
	Other road, drive or track

Unfenced roads and tracks are shown by pecked lines

.... Path

RAILWAYS

——————	Multiple track } Standard gauge
—·—·—·—	Single track }
—+—+—+—	Narrow gauge
	Siding
	Cutting
	Embankment
—(::::::)—	Tunnel
	Road over & under
	Level crossing, station

PUBLIC RIGHTS OF WAY

- - - - - - - }	Public paths {	Footpath
— — — — — }		Bridleway
—·—·—·—·—	Road used as a public path	

DANGER AREA —
MOD ranges in the area
Danger!
Observe warning notices

Public rights of way indicated by these symbols have been derived from Definitive Maps as amended by later enactments or instruments held by Ordnance Survey and are shown subject to the limitations imposed by the scale of mapping
The representation on this map of any other road, track or path is no evidence of the existence of a right of way

BOUNDARIES

—·—·—·—	County
— — — —	District
....	Civil Parish
— — — — —	Constituency (County or Borough)

} Coincident boundaries are shown by the first appropriate symbol opposite

*For Ordnance Survey purposes County Boundary is deemed to be the limit of the parish structure whether or not a parish area adjoins

SYMBOLS

♦ } Church	with tower	
♦ } or	with spire	
+ } chapel	without tower or spire	
▨ ▲	Glasshouse, Youth hostel	
⬗	Bus or coach station	
� ⊥ Λ	Lighthouse, lightship, beacon	
△	Triangulation station	
♦ ♦ ·:· } Triangulation	church, chapel,	
☥ Λ } point on	lighthouse, beacon,	
⬚ ⊙ }	building & chimney	
° BP, BS	Boundary Post, Stone	
· T, A, R	Telephone, public, AA, RAC	
P, ·MP, MS	Post office, Mile Post, Stone	

VILLA	Roman antiquity (AD 43 to AD 420)
Castle	Other antiquities
⊹	Site of antiquity
⚔ 1066	Site of battle (with date)
	Gravel pit
	Sand pit
	Chalk pit, clay pit or quarry
	Refuse or slag heap
▰▰▰	Sloping masonry
· W, Spr	Well, Spring

☐	Water
☐	Sand, sand & shingle
☐	Mud
	NT	National Trust always open
	NT	National Trust opening restricted

Electricity transmission line
pylon   pole

VEGETATION

Limits of vegetation are defined by positioning of the symbols but may be delineated also by pecks or dots

♣ ♣	Coniferous trees	ᵒᵃ ᵒᵃ	Scrub		Reeds
○ ○	Non-coniferous trees	·ᵗ· ·ᵗ·	Bracken, rough grassland	} Shown collectively as rough grassland on some sheets	
	Coppice	In some areas bracken (") and rough grassland (······) are shown separately			Marsh
∘ ∘ ∘	Orchard	······	Heath		Saltings

HEIGHTS AND ROCK FEATURES

50 · } Determined { ground survey
285 · } by { air survey

Surface heights are to the nearest metre above mean sea level. Heights shown close to a triangulation pillar refer to the station height at ground level and not necessarily to the summit

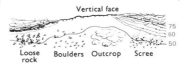

Vertical face

Loose rock   Boulders   Outcrop   Scree

75
60
50

Contours are at 5 metres vertical interval

The symbols shown below appear only on first series OS maps which are used on maps 29,30,31, 32 and 33, and part of maps 5,7,8,28,34,35,37,41,42 and 43.

Footpaths	FP / Fenced FP / Unfenced
Public Buildings	Glasshouses
National Trust Area	*Sheen Common NT*	Orchard
	Furze
Osier Bed	Rough Pasture Heath & Moor
Reeds	Marsh
Park, Fenced	Well .... W o
Wood, Coniferous, Fenced	Spring .... Spr o
	Wind Pump .... Wd Pp .
Wood, Non-Coniferous Unfenced	Contours are at 25 feet vertical interval.
Brushwood, Fenced & Unfenced	Spot Height .... 123 ·

NORTH DOWNS WAY

—·—·— PERMISSIVE ROUTE

— — — — TEMPORARY ROUTE

•••••••••••• PROPOSED ROUTE

The North Downs Way opens up one of the best known but, for all that, most neglected natural attractions of the South East. How many times have I sped through the chalk-faced gaps, en route to the south coast or the Continent, oblivious of the pleasures that abound there? Or have gone north, to the Pennines, or west to the coastal paths, in search of lung-filling adventure? The North Downs Way may be gentle, easy meat in the muscular sense, but it is immensely varied, and the views across the Weald are English in the most idyllic sense. I shall certainly walk it again.

This book has been made possible by a group of helpful nature lovers — I mention John Ashdown and Evelyn Farrant from the Kent County Council, Dennis Rice from

Surrey County Council and Foster Summerson, now with the Department of the Environment. Many others participated — and still do — in keeping the Way up to scratch. Thanks also to Nigel Davies, conservation warden at Ranmore Common, for his enthusiastic conversations on the flora and fauna of chalk grassland.

One word of partial defence. I have used 'his' throughout the text, when 'her' could equally well apply. In the absence of a suitable non-sexist pronoun, there is no alternative. But I recall seeing rather more women walking the downs than men.

Finally, I hope this book helps to get you out of the house, away from that television screen and on your Way.

D.H.

Introduction

The chalk downs which rise above Surrey and Kent, all the way to the Channel, are one of the most ancient arteries of communication in Britain. The first permanent settlers, who arrived 6,000 years ago, followed this high road above the impenetrable forests of the Weald. So did the Romans, and then Christians on the pilgrimage to Thomas à Becket's shrine at Canterbury Cathedral. With the appearance of the railway and then the motor car, the paths along these downs — as with paths all over the country — were used less and less. Until, earlier this century, we discovered the attractions of the English countryside and took to walking it for our pleasure and leisure.

After the Second World War, the National Parks and Access to the Countryside Act established the National Parks Commission (later to become the Countryside Commission) as the instrument for setting up long-distance paths. There are now 12 long-distance paths in England and Wales, the Pennine Way being the first. In September 1978 the then Archbishop of Canterbury, Dr. Donald Coggan, officially opened the North Downs Way, from Farnham in Surrey to Dover, with an alternative loop through Canterbury.

A glance at the map will show that one of the striking aspects of the North Downs Way is its nearness to London, where a vast concentration of city dwellers is bursting for an excursion into the countryside. The Way is intercepted by a good network of railways, buses and roads, making it easily accessible to Londoners, as well as to the people of Kent, Surrey and Sussex.

The description of the Way is from west to east. But the route is carefully waymarked and can, of course, be walked in either direction. There are those who will wish to walk the North Downs Way at one go or over three or more weekends; or perhaps every Sunday afternoon in the course of one summer. I have tried to divide the book in such a way as to allow for every sort of variation.

The chapters on the path are divided into 10 stages, three of which are entirely in Surrey, the fourth is in border country, the next four go through Kent to Dover, while the

River Wey, near Farnham

last two account for the 51-kilometre pilgrims' route through Canterbury. The stages are admittedly uneven, with the first, to Guildford, only 17¾ kilometres, while it is twice the distance from Wye to Dover. This is necessary because in some places accommodation, whether bed and breakfast, youth hostels, cheap hotels, and even camping, is fairly scant, so that transport to and from the Way becomes an important factor.

The stages average out at 24 kilometres a day. If this does not fit the age, health, or rambling philosophy of the reader, I can recommend a slower pace, demanding about 15 kilometres a day. The route would then be:

1	Farnham — Guildford	17¾ kilometres
2	Guildford — Ranmore Common (near Dorking)	
		35 kilometres
3	to Reigate Hill	51 kilometres
4	to South Hawke (near Oxted)	69 kilometres
5	to Knockholt Pound	81 kilometres
6	to Wrotham	97 kilometres
7	to M2 bridge west	111 kilometres
8	to Detling	127 kilometres
9	to Charing	141 kilometres
	or to Lenham	148 kilometres
10	to Wye	160 kilometres
11	to Etchinghill	177 kilometres
12	to Dover	195 kilometres

Section via Canterbury

13	Boughton Lees to Canterbury	20 kilometres
14	to Woolage Village	35 kilometres
15	to Dover	51 kilometres

Countryside ranger at work on the North Downs Way

Those who need to fly the course can devise their own timetables. Farnham to Dover in six days; or the Dover–Canterbury–Dover 90-kilometre triangle over a long summer weekend?

The North Downs Way keeps almost entirely within two Areas of Outstanding Natural Beauty (AONBs), the Surrey Hills and the Kent Downs. These areas have been specially designated for conservation purposes, though their popularity can be self-defeating, as is evident from the most fleeting passage across the day-tripper land of Box Hill.

The Way also crosses the Wye and Crundale Downs National Nature Reserve and enters or skirts a number of Sites of Special Scientific Interest (SSSIs) and National Nature Reserves (NNRs). Here the Nature Conservancy Council is doing its best to preserve rare and endangered habitats, like the chalk grassland of the Wye and Crundale Downs. Rare wildlife communities — plants, animals, butterflies — are also on the Council's protected list.

As with its sister South Downs Way, this route keeps to the Weald side of the downs, for most of the journey at least. We are thus on the south side, and so benefit from the sunnier route. Only on the Canterbury to Dover section do we leave the Weald for the north side of the downs. But don't think that this is a perennially mild, dependable climate. In winter, thick snow can cover the path. The mist comes in fast from the sea, and night falls without benefit of moon or stars. You can get lost.

So make sure you have a compass, whistle, foil blanket, water bottle, first-aid kit, waterproof torch, a warm sweater and spare socks, in addition to lightweight mac and leggings, and boots that will keep your feet dry.

Cover your head in cold/hot weather to avoid heat loss/sunstroke. A scarf round the neck keeps off wind and sunburn. And don't forget the spare specs.

The North Downs Way is a modern route and is not based on the Pilgrims' Way, although at times they do converge. The exact line of the pilgrims' route is not always certain, though we do know that for the most part it followed the line below the ridge of the downs. Today much of it is metalled, and so unpleasant walking. The North Downs Way follows the actual ridge of the downs whenever it can.

The Pilgrims' Way begins at Winchester, where the North Downs have their origins. The Countryside Commission's forerunner, the National Parks Commission, did briefly consider starting the North Downs Way at Winchester as well, and the Ramblers' Association did a survey of a possible route in the 1950s. But there was nothing suitably rustic — the paths either went on or next to a metalled road — and the idea was dropped. The Commission also considered linking up with the Ridgeway Path, north-east from Farnham to Inkpen Beacon, but decided against, and that is now unlikely to be implemented. The Way is crossed by other, unofficial,

3

long-distance paths, like the Weald Way (Gravesend, Uck-field to Eastbourne) and the Saxon Shore Way round Kent.

The fact that the North Downs Way is a new path has meant that in many places fresh rights of way have had to be negotiated. Sometimes these are speedily arranged, but occasionally there are hitches. Though the line of the path has been approved, there are some stretches which are not yet open to the public. The most important of these is four kilometres from Detling to Broad Street (near Hollingbourne) where a right of way on the down is under negotiation. And at Guildford the bridge across the Wey is still awaited, necessitating a diversion of nearly one kilometre. There is also a temporary route near Wrotham and at Dean, above Folkestone.

The North Downs Way is well enough waymarked for the rawest beginner to follow. The tell-tale acorn, emblem of the Countryside Commission's long-distance paths, marks the way: in Surrey, on a wooden post; in Kent, on a stone plinth. Local groups have in places helped the doubting Thomases with a yellow plastic arrow attached to a tree or stile.

Waymarks in Surrey . . .   . . . and Kent

Might I make one suggestion, even though it will be self-evident for the established practitioner of the outdoors? The North Downs Way is a fascinating journey through much of southern England, and though it crosses several motorways and heavily used dual carriageways, it always hurries back to a pleasant rusticity. But it is, in the current jargon, more than just a pretty face. Why not pursue, or commence, an outdoor hobby, like wild flower or tree spotting? Each speciality has at least one book which can be pocketed without being too much of a burden. Butterfly observing (but, please, not collecting), church architecture, cloud formation, Chaucer's England, even grasses, are all suitable cases for study, as is that most popular of all outdoor 'collecting', bird-watching, for which a pair of binoculars is essential. In such a way, you will add an extra dimension to your walk.

A final word. This guide book is what it says it is, a guide. It is not a travelogue, for which there are specific books available. I have more often tried to describe the Way as 'passing under a pylon' (which is a permanent fixture) rather than 'to the left of a horse' (which is not guaranteed to be standing there five minutes later). But descriptions and comments on the condition of the path are influenced by the season of the year. Thus the early part was walked in July, and I ended the last eight kilometres from Waldershare Park into Dover on a breezy Sunday in November.

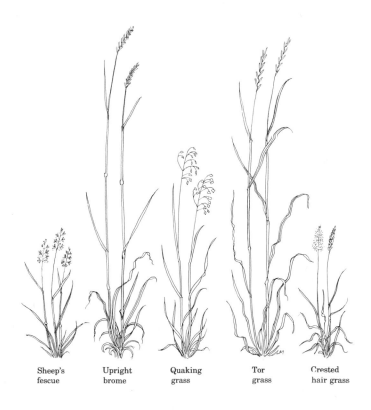

| Sheep's | Upright | Quaking | Tor | Crested |
| fescue | brome | grass | grass | hair grass |

The walker and the law

The North Downs Way was a top priority undertaking, envisaged, created and launched in a combined operation by the Countryside Commission and the Kent and Surrey County Councils. In addition, Ramblers' Association groups and community organisations representing a wide range of interests have helped make it a veritable walker's paradise, easy to follow and continuous.

Well, almost continuous, for even the North Downs Way has occasional problems. In one field, a bull grazes menacingly from his stance right on the very path. Elsewhere, a farmer has not yet agreed to terms for opening up a four-kilometre section, so that at times the walker must plod through stubble and ploughed fields at the bottom of the downs. And sometimes, on paths which are not bridleways, horses' hooves mar the walker's enjoyment.

Problems like these are more widespread on local paths where the very existence of a right of way may be contested by a farmer and where the local council refuses to live up to its responsibilities. But the law is the same whether it relates to the North Downs Way or to a mucky traipse across a beetroot patch.

It is well to remember that there is no part of Britain which is not owned by some person or organisation. The path, and the adjacent fields or woods, no matter how unclaimed and open they may seem, do belong to Farmer Jones, or the county council, the Crown, the National Trust, the Forestry Commission, British Rail, a quarrying company. (Though the county council, as the highway authority, is normally taken to 'own' the actual surface of the path.)

Not all paths are public rights of way. They can be private paths open only to a farmer and his employees, or, in a forest, to employees of the Forestry Commission. We are here talking about *public* footpaths and bridleways. They are just as much a highway as the Old Kent Road.

While we and our dogs may walk on both footpath and bridleway, horses and pedal bicycles are restricted to the latter. Cyclists, incidentally, must give way to horse-riders and walkers on bridleways, while a motorist who drives a car

7

on to a footpath or bridleway without permission is liable to a fine of £10.

We ascertain whether a footpath or bridleway is a right of way by consulting the definitive map of the area, which all county councils in England and Wales are obliged to draw up. The map is available for inspection at the offices of county councils, district councils and often the parish clerk. Every footpath and bridleway has a number, sometimes seen on signposts on the North Downs Way. These maps are supposed to be revised every five years, so that there is a continuing process of adding fresh paths and extinguishing others from the official record. In practice, most maps are years out of date.

A path can be public even if not on the definitive map. Then, it must have been used, and regarded, as a public right of way without challenge for 20 years.

The law also provides for the creation of a path through the formal dedication by the landowner to public use. In practice, this does not happen very often. In the case of long-distance paths, where existing paths need to be joined up, the intervening sections might be the subject of a creation agreement between the landowner and the highway author-ity. In this way an existing private path would become public or a completely fresh track would be created.

If no agreement is reached, the last resort is a compulsory order made subject to the consent of the Secretary of State for the Environment or for Wales. This solution would invari-ably require a public inquiry, and is rarely used.

But what happens if, while out walking, we find the path is obstructed? If it is a lorry or a pile of manure, we will go round. A locked gate, and we will climb over. By law we may remove only as much of the obstruction (e.g. barbed wire fence) as is necessary to continue on our way. But it must be a bona fide journey — setting out with the express intention of challenging the wayward landowner could have both crimi-nal and civil law consequences. That takes us into the realm of political protest! There are other less dramatic ways of overcoming obstacles. The county council has a duty to keep public paths clear, though this is often delegated to the district council. When a thwarted rambler reports the obstruction, the council should order its removal, failing which, do the work itself and send the bill to the landowner.

It is also the duty of the highway authority to keep the path in a good enough state of repair to allow passage in all seasons. (The Countryside Commission foots the bill for maintaining long-distance paths like the North Downs Way.) Natural vegetation should be cleared from a footpath, while overhanging plants and branches may have to be removed to allow the path to dry out after rain. The highway authority is liable for injuries resulting from the unrepaired path. It is for the rambler to report broken stiles or dangerous paths to the local council.

Which leads us to one of the most vexing sources of dispute between farmers and ramblers — the ploughing up of a path running through a field. Remember that you must stick to the official line of the path and *not* walk round the field. The farmer usually does have the right to cultivate the entire field provided he gives the local council a week's notice. After ploughing, he must make good the surface of the path within six weeks from giving notice, or within three weeks of the actual ploughing if he has failed to give notice. Most farmers simply roll out the furrows and leave it at that. Rarely, the farmer may be allowed to make a diversion for a three-month period, but the start and finish must be signposted — and the diversion indicated.

If matters have gone so far that crops are growing on the path, we should still follow the line of the path. The law provides a swingeing fine of £200 for not restoring the surface adequately.

From the foregoing, it is clear that the law is more interested in the behaviour of farmers than of path users. But the rambler and rider do have important responsibilities, both legal and moral. Thus we should avoid making fires (except where permitted, and that is not often on the North Downs Way), letting dogs run free where animals are pasturing, picking wild flowers, tampering with waymarks — and also take steps to see that others behave as well. This might amount to anything from raising a censorious eyebrow at the miscreant to making a report to a warden or police station. In most cases, common sense will help to decide on the best action.

A note on that misleading discourager *Trespassers will be prosecuted*. Only when property is damaged is there a criminal offence of trespass. If, however, a walker deliberately uses the footpath to make life uncomfortable for the landowner — by, for instance, making faces at people inside the house — there could be grounds for a civil action. Where the walker steps off the footpath he is on more dangerous ground, though still not breaking the law. But the landowner may take action in the civil courts, and if he wins, would recover costs. If property were damaged, there would be grounds for a prosecution.

There remains the final and vital consideration of the extinction of public paths. It is a myth that rights of way are lost if paths are not used for 20 years. The maxim is clear — *Once a highway, always a highway*. Only an order made under statute law by the local authority can deprive a path of its public access. This elaborate operation is designed to give path users the benefit of the doubt. The council makes the 'order' closing the path, which it might consider no longer needed for public use. Making the order does not automatically close the path. It must be published in the *London Gazette* and a local newspaper, as well as posted at both ends of the doomed section. If there are no objections within 28 days, the path is closed. If there are, the Department of the Environment will set up an inquiry. The same process is followed for a diversion of a path.

Walking in the countryside is the nation's most favoured outdoor leisure activity. There are 190,000 kilometres of public footpaths and bridleways in England and Wales. Yet every year about 800 kilometres of paths are lost. In the last resort, this unique national asset has to be protected by those who enjoy it. We cannot be too fussy, too daring, too thick-skinned in its defence. The law, wisely used, is our most effective weapon.

For a more detailed study, I can recommend *A Practical Guide to the Law of Footpaths and Bridleways,* published by the Commons, Open Spaces and Footpaths Preservation Society, 25A Bell Street, Henley-on-Thames, Oxon. The Ramblers' Association pamphlet *Right of Way* is a concise point-by-point guide.

Pilgrims at Canterbury from a 15th-century manuscript

The Garden of England and the Stockbroker Belt

The North Downs bisect two south-eastern counties of England, Kent and Surrey. This spinal column of downs unites two counties which are, for the most part, unalike. Differences are reflected not only in our image of them — the Garden of England, the Stockbroker Belt — but in their history, urban and rural landscape, agriculture, architecture, relationship to London and, in the case of the maritime Kent, in its openness to both invader and trader from across the Channel.

Surrey
'Surrey' means the people of the southern region, originating from 'Suthridge', those middle Saxons who also ruled farther north in Middlesex. A vague, misty beginning, hardly the stuff of local patriotism, such as we find in Yorkshire, Dorset or Kent. Surrey suffers from an identity problem.

Surrey is small — 1,600 square kilometres, 65 kilometres across, almost 40 deep to the Sussex border — and, with one million inhabitants, thickly populated in parts. It is really two counties, divided by the downs — the north, London's underbelly, is 15 kilometres of flat Surrey plain, which commuters have rendered virtually indistinguishable from the suburbs of London.

This northern half has shrunk considerably in the last century, due to the consolidation of the metropolis. In Victorian times Surrey included much of the right bank of London's Thames. But in 1889, with the formation of the London County Council, a sizeable chunk was lost, including the Surrey Docks and Brixton — which was one of the 'hundreds' recorded in the Domesday Book — and the Oval cricket ground in Kennington, still the county's main stadium.

With the coming of the Greater London Council in 1965, out went Richmond, Wimbledon, Croydon, even Kew Gardens. And though Guildford, the county town, remains safely within Surrey's confines, County Hall is still at Kingston upon Thames, now a London borough. For all that, Surrey has not been as badly emasculated as Middlesex by local government reorganisation. Surrey, in fact, gained several towns and a 25-kilometre stretch of the Thames at Middlesex's expense.

Beyond the downs is another face of the county, the Weald (or 'Wild'), thickly wooded in many places, with winding roads across the clay to isolated farm and hamlet, and some fairly big towns where the rivers have pierced the wall of chalk. Parts are commuter belt, like Godstone or Dorking, but even these have retained an integrity despite the nearness of Victoria Station. We have the Green Belt legislation to thank. Coming on the eve of the last war, it saved Surrey in particular from the excesses of overspill and dormitory planning. But in addition to the ever-thickening road traffic, aircraft noise from Heathrow and Gatwick, the international airports on its borders, intrudes just about everywhere.

Surrey, thanks to its constantly evolving geology, has a varied landscape. Starting in the low-lying north, there is London clay, then the limestone hills, 15 kilometres wide at the Kent border, less than one kilometre as the Hog's Back enters Hampshire. Then clay-topped chalk, lined by a thin strip of gault clay (as in the Vale of Holmesdale), then lower greensand, which fattens where the chalk is thin in the west, and all but disappears where it thickens (the highest point in the South East — Leith Hill, 294 metres — is of greensand) and finally the heavy uncompromising clay of the Weald.

Clay is not the best soil for cereals, so that dairy and mixed farming are a feature of the Weald. Farms are medium sized, about 80 to 120 hectares, and usually family owned, unlike the tenant farmers of Sussex. The market gardening tradition goes as close to London as Vauxhall, though these days houses and factories have pushed horticulture out along the light sandy soil of the Bagshot sands, to Woking, Camberley, Guildford, as far as the New Forest. It is said that some of the most fertile soil in England lies at the bottom of the runways at Heathrow Airport. The Bagshot area concentrates on hardy nursery stock — rose bushes, conifers, magnolias — as opposed to glasshouse cultivation. The Royal Horticultural Society gardens and testing grounds are at Wisley.

Surrey's natural resources do not supply the best material for fine building. After the Conquest, much of the county was given to William's half brother, Odo of Bayeux, but he built no Norman castles. Churches are small though, as we see from our walk, there are gems among them. But the county was without a cathedral until Guildford's was consecrated in 1962. Surrey remained rural and remote until the dissolution of the monasteries in the sixteenth century, and then it became a magnet for Londoners. Private families moved in and built some fine stately homes. One of them, Loseley House, is seen from the Way.

Surrey also became a byword for commuter living, a stockbroker belt with manicured gardens lining the approaches to the capital. As Ian Nairn points out in *The*

Buildings of England, 'A history of English medieval architecture could be written without once mentioning a surviving Surrey building; a history of the suburb or folly could almost be written without once going outside the county.'

Despite the nearness of London, several towns have flourishing theatres, their names taken from famous actors — the Yvonne Arnaud at Guildford, the Ashcroft at Croydon, the Thorndyke at Leatherhead and the Redgrave at Farnham.

But we must not think that Surrey is devoid of history. It was at Runnymede, near modern Egham, that the barons twisted King John's arm into signing Magna Carta in 1215. A century and a half later, the Peasants' Revolt, in which labourers from all the home counties, led by Wat Tyler from Kent, briefly took over London. Jack Cade, a Surrey man by adoption, led the 1450 rebellion.

Further back, however, when Surrey did not exist as an entity, there was a pagan Saxon cemetery at Guildford, and before that, Roman villas at Farnham and at Titsey, which also had a temple and a pottery. Surrey's place on the pre-Christian Harroway ('Hard Way') along the downs to Salisbury and Stonehenge accounts for these prehistoric finds — a Bronze Age urn cemetery near Farnham, and the earliest preserved dwelling site in England, from the mesolithic (Middle Stone Age) period, at Abinger. For all that, it is not a county rich in archaeological remains.

Kent

Kent is an altogether different county — self-contained, its origins traceable to the dawn of English history. Indeed, the Swanscombe man, whose skull was found near Gravesend, dates back 300,000 years. After that, the ice advanced and receded across southern England and we pick up relics of the mesolithic hunter 12 millenniums ago. (He probably came on foot, for Britain was part of the European mainland as late as 5,000 BC.) Flint instruments, fashioned from the stone found in abundance in the top layers of the chalk, have been discovered in many downland sites.

It was then that Kent established itself, willy-nilly, because of its geographical placing, as the stepping-stone between Britain and much of the Continent. New Stone Age men (neolithic), our first farmers, brought and planted wheat and barley in light downs soil and along the Darent and other rivers (today these cereals account for more than three-quarters of Britain's arable land). They buried their dead in tombs like the one at Kit's Coty House, above the Medway. Then, from the Rhineland, came a people working with a new material, bronze. Pits near Birchington, on the Isle of Thanet, have yielded a large bronze hoard, as well as pottery.

Iron tools and weapons date from the sixth century BC, and hill forts from the period existed at places like Bigbury (near Canterbury), at Ightham, and at Hulberry near Lullingstone. It was the early beginning of a tradition only recently disappeared. Iron foundries and their hammer ponds later became a major Wealden industry.

A constant stream of settlers were attracted like bees to

Flint axe-heads, unpolished (left) and polished

Kit's Coty House burial chamber

the honey-pot of Kent. A Belgian tribe called (by the Romans) *Cantii,* arrived just over 2,000 years ago, giving their name to the county and its best known town, called *Durovernum* by the Romans, but *Cantwarabyrig* by the Saxons. They were probably responsible for laying part of the track which is now the North Downs Way. Thanks to a plough capable of working the heavier clay soil, they could move farther away from the downs. They exported corn and cattle to Europe.

Julius Caesar was one of the two most celebrated visitors in the county annals. It is fitting that the beginnings of recorded history should coincide with reports of how the all-conquering Roman general received a less than hospitable welcome. In 55 BC his armada was repelled by the *Belgae* at Deal, but a year later the local tribes succumbed — though it was not for another century that the Roman occupation began in earnest. They built roads (the Way crosses Watling Street) and introduced apples and cherries. One of the finest of the 40 Roman remains in Kent is the villa at Lullingstone, in the Darent Valley.

St. Augustine was the other well-remembered visitor. In 596 he set about reorganising the church in England with himself as the first Archbishop of Canterbury. By then Kent was a prosperous kingdom under Ethelbert, whose wife,

Bertha, daughter of the Frankish king of Paris, was already a Christian.

After Hastings, William the Conqueror had to proceed to London via Dover, such was the denseness of the Weald. And as he did not actually conquer Kent, the county has felt itself free to use *Invicta* (undefeated) as its motto. The Normans brought feudalism, but at least Kent was prosperous, thanks to the fertile soil. Large tracts of the county were owned by the church. After the dissolution of the monasteries, castles — at Sandown, Walmer, Deal — were built in case of a papist invasion. But the Spanish Armada (1588) did not quite make it, so that the next (peaceful) invasion was by Protestant Flemings, fleeing persecution, bringing hops and the art of weaving.

Once again, after the French Revolution, invasion fever wracked England. The Martello towers and the Grand Military Canal, an expensive folly built along Romney Marsh, remain today. The invasion never came. But in the Second World War, though the Germans did not cross the Channel, 3,000 people in Kent were killed by cross-Channel shelling from the coast of France.

The invasion has come from within. The Georgian period saw the construction of turnpike roads, paid for by tolls (turnpike being another word for tollgate), after which road surfaces improved enormously. Fruit and vegetables could be more easily shifted to London; the garden (Kent) was from now on to serve the house (London). The railways followed, then the motorways to the Channel so that today Kent is more than ever a springboard to and from Europe.

Geology, vegetation and architecture are all closely inter-linked, and nowhere more so than in Kent. In general, the London clay, gault, chalk, more gault, lower greensand, and finally, Weald clay, cover the county southwards as they do in Surrey. In the south, Royal Tunbridge Wells and the alluvial flatness of Romney Marsh recall the days when the sea bit deeply into Kent.

These materials are seen throughout. Chalk, though not durable as a building stone, does possess lime for plaster. But the flint found in chalk is to be seen in the city walls of Canterbury. It is not pretty, but lasts and lasts, standing up well against the corrosion of the sea air. Bricks and tiles, yellow and pink from gault, red from the Weald, are products of clay. There is a fourteenth-century tile yard at Old Naccolt, near Wye. The tiles are so good that thatch is rarely used in Kent.

And from greensand — which is rarely green and seldom sand — and the Hythe Beds around Maidstone in particular, comes the Kentish ragstone, used by the Romans for the walls of *Londinium* and by the Victorians for London churches.

Oak has also played its role, as witness the plethora of Wealden houses, timber-framed yeoman farmers' cottages.

15th-century Wealden house

The description is slightly misleading, for they are by no means confined to the Weald, and in Kent most are found near Maidstone. These distinctive structures had halls open to the roof, a central hearth, and a second storey at one end, with bedrooms above the kitchen and solar (living room). The upper storey jettied out on projecting beams, and this overhang was a peculiar attribute of the Wealden house. En route, the best example is the sixteenth-century Old Bell Farm at Harrietsham.

The oast-house represents agricultural building at its most unusual and picturesque. This system of drying hops involves a brick kiln under a sloping roof with a cowl at the top to provide a good draught. The earliest (sixteenth century) were oblong, later square, then, from 1800, round, which were misguidedly thought to provide better heat distribution. Now most have been converted into quaint homes while the hops dry out in unassuming barns.

But, above all else, Kent is famed for its apples. There was a time when the orchards consisted of scraggy old trees, scattered higgledy-piggledy, and lovely to climb at your leisure.

There were, literally, dozens of dessert and cooking varieties ... Beauty of Bath, Red Astrachan, Devonshire Quarrenden, Melba, Peasgood's Nonsuch, Orleans Reinette,

Bramley's Seedling

Grenadier   Tydeman's Early

Cox's   Worcester

Orange Pippin   Discovery   Pearmain

Laxton's Superb   Crispin

                    Egremont Russet

Tom Putt (not all of these from Kent). In the late summer and autumn, gipsies, students, cockney workers on paid holidays, wives from Maidstone earning pocket money, came to harvest the crop.

Even before Britain joined the European Community, competition from southern France and northern Italy was biting into the market. Fruit farmers had to modernise or die. Old trees were grubbed out and when not put under the plough the orchards were replanted in orderly fashion, usually with trees whose highest fruit was no taller than a man standing on a box can reach. Itinerant workers have become largely redundant. But most important, the industry is concentrating on 10 or so apples, headed by Kent's finest, the Cox's Orange Pippin. (The others are Tydeman's Early, Discovery, Egremont Russet, Crispin, Laxton's Superb and Worcester Pearmain, plus the cookers, Grenadier and Bramley's Seedling.) It is now possible that though there are fewer orchards in Kent and the other apple counties the volume of fruit grown is greater. Kent's orchards may not be as pretty as they used to be, but they are keeping the English apple business alive.

The Way passes close to the Kent collieries east of Canterbury. Good coking coal has been mined since the turn of the century, but four pits have been closed down, leaving Tilmanstone, Betteshanger and Snowdown, though the Coal Board has announced that this last is uneconomic and might have to close as well.

Kent, with a population of more than one and a half million, has surprisingly few big towns. Canterbury has a mere 35,000 inhabitants, as has Dover. The Medway towns number 200,000 and the largest is the county town, Maidstone, with over 70,000. Twice the size of Surrey, considerably more rural, Kent has managed to survive more happily its nearness to the capital and to retain an impressive independence laced with local patriotism.

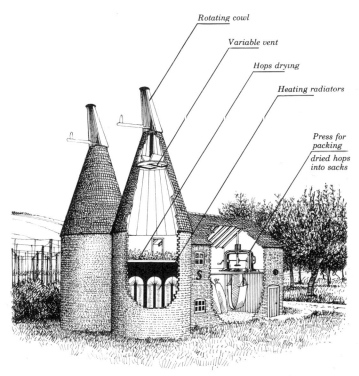

Rotating cowl

Variable vent

Hops drying

Heating radiators

Press for packing dried hops into sacks

Inside an oast-house

The where, how and what of chalk downs

To describe downs simply as chalk covered with springy grass is much like saying that the Mona Lisa is paint and canvas. Downs do, or did, have the basic elements of chalk and grass, but they also vary enormously in geology, wildlife and their treatment by man.

Imagine a piece of seaweed floating in a still rock pool, its branches running from a central knot, sometimes above, sometimes below the surface of the water. Salisbury Plain and the Marlborough Downs are that knot, centred in Wiltshire, but jutting into Berkshire and Hampshire. North-eastwards, the chalk ridge runs along the Berkshire Downs, dropping at the Goring Gap where it is pierced by the Thames, then into the Chilterns, becoming hardly visible in East Anglia until reaching the coastal cliffs of north Norfolk. Beyond the Wash are the Lincolnshire Wolds and finally, jumping the Humber, the Wolds of the East Riding of Yorkshire, plunging magnificently into the sea at Bempton and Flamborough Head.

South-westwards, the ridge runs above Hardy's Blackmoor Vale and Cranborne Chase, to Toller Down Gate via the Dorset Downs. The chalk sinks, to reappear beyond Lyme Regis at Beer Head. The Isle of Wight also has a chalk ridge, separated from the south coast by the Hampshire Basin.

The third ridge leaving the central knot forms the South Downs, which run into the sea at Beachy Head. A fourth ridge veins along the Newbury Downs, the highest of the chalk hills, then by a depression between Basingstoke and Farnham, where the steep scarp of the Hog's Back begins the North Downs' journey to the white cliffs of Dover.

In the cretaceous period (130 million to 60 million years ago) when dinosaurs roamed the land, myriads of minute sea shells, plankton and other microscopic life were dropping on to the sea-bed. This was an inland sea, stretching over much of north-west and central Europe. In time, a white calcareous sediment, 300 metres and more thick in places, formed under the water, at the rate of 30 centimetres every 30,000 years. This chalky limestone was pure at the top, mixed with other materials lower down.

The sea-bed began to rise, gently it is thought, and over a

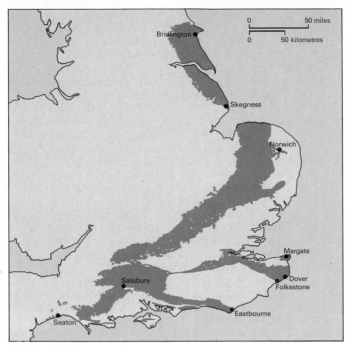

Britain's chalklands

period of millions of years, the same earth movement that shaped the Alps, so forming a vast dome over much of south-east England and northern France, including the Channel. There were smaller domes, above the Vale of Pewsey and in the south of the Isle of Wight.

In time, wind and rain tore into the dome and the rivers pierced holes in the chalk, and a new drainage pattern emerged. Eventually, the chalk cap of the dome wore away, exposing gault clay and older sandstones and clays in the topsy-turvy landscape of the Weald. But the chalk crust of the dome survived, in the form of the North and South Downs.

Had the oozy sediment remained long enough at the sea bottom to harden into limestone — chalk is simply friable limestone — then Kent and Surrey would have been counties of rugged uplands with high-rise fells reminiscent of the north Pennines.

Instead, the dip slope falls gently on the outer edges of the dome. The inner scarp, south facing in the case of the North Downs, is steeper, but rarely too much so for a direct ascent. For downs are of modest proportions, even by English standards, the tallest of all, Walbury Hill in Berkshire, being lower than 300 metres. When, occasionally, the gentle undulations are italicised by abrupt, even dangerous, precipices, it is through the action of the quarrymen, or, as at

Folkestone, of the sea. One special feature of the downs is the dry river valleys, which no longer carry water. During the Ice Age, when the normally permeable chalk froze and could not act as a drain, melting water careered off the hillside in the spring thaw, carrying chalky sludge, like porridge.

Chalk is not commonly used as an external building material, though there are exceptions, as with the base of the east face of Guildford Castle. It is too soft, being particularly vulnerable to frost and sea air. The chalk quarries which pockmark the North Downs Way for its entire distance are almost all disused today. The soft chalk was once used for plaster, or more commonly for making agricultural lime. The lime kilns above Brockham and Betchworth are a reminder of those days, before the industry moved to the hard dry limestone of the Peak District.

The softest chalk is found at the base of the downs escarpment up to about the level of the Pilgrims' Way, and is often covered by hill-wash or sludge. But it is the upper chalk, a soft white limestone laced with flint and found on the dip slope of the downs (as at Betsom's Hill), which has made an important contribution to local architecture. Flint may not be elegant, but it certainly is durable, and so has been used in church and domestic building as an antidote to corrosion near the sea and to the weather on the northern reaches of the North Downs.

These days, it is ironic that most of the diggings on the North Downs are for plain old builder's gravel.

Whitethroat

Bullfinch

Hawthorn

Magpie

Bramble

Traveller's joy

Buckthorn

Linnet

Hedgehog

Deadly
nightshade

Adder

Marjoram

24

Common shrew

Chalk grassland:
the struggle for survival

An outing along unimproved chalk grassland is a pleasure not to be missed. The grass is warm and dry, and its springiness, like the turf of a bowling green, provides hours of effortless walking. Surely it is the best piece of external carpeting in Europe? The grassland was formed some 8,000 years ago in post-glacial Britain. Beech and, on the steeper slopes, yew, flourished, until neolithic farmers cleared the woods for habitation and farming. It is safe to say that sheep have grazed these downs for 5,000 years. And from that cultivation arose a habitat as delightful as it is unique.

It is this fescue grass, or sheep's fescue, which gives chalk downs their unique sward. The grass is constantly cropped by grazing sheep and nibbling rabbit. Under this tight grazing régime no plant dominates, because all are bitten off impartially. There is no competition for light, water, nutrients, or whatever is necessary for survival, for all are equal — a sort of plant socialism. There can be 50 different species of plant to a square metre of grass — orchids, cowslip, hairy violet, marjoram, thyme, horseshoe vetch and many others in a colourful and busy tapestry.

Insects depend on these flowers for survival. The dark green fritillary butterfly is not uncommon, but the caterpillar needs to feed on the hairy violet to complete its life-cycle. The rare Adonis blue, which now breeds in only 80 colonies in the whole country, must have horseshoe vetch. The interrelationship of life on the chalk grassland is illustrated by one of its most numerous inhabitants, the yellow meadow ant. Their big mounds are a common feature of the habitat, and some have been there for 200 years. Green woodpeckers feed on the ants, as do badgers, which have a way of ripping into the nest and grubbing for their dinner.

Today, undisturbed chalk grassland is vanishing at an alarming rate. Some would say that, apart from occasional 'museums', it has already disappeared. The rot began to set in two centuries ago, when large portions of grassland in southern England previously grazed by sheep were given over to corn production. And when England was almost cut off by Napoleon, the need for self-sufficiency in food accelerated this process. Still, that agricultural revolution left vast areas of the chalk downland as it always had been.

From the 1930s, however, sheep were removed in progressively greater numbers from even the more virginal slopes of the downs. And in 1954, the great myxomatosis plague decimated the country's rabbit population. With these two industrious short-back-and-sides barbers gone, the thinning process stopped. Now, all the ham actors who had been waiting in the wings stepped on stage. Tor, an unpalatable grass which crossed from the Continent in the last 100 years, asserted itself in many areas, while the smaller plants and grasses were unceremoniously shoved aside in this new struggle for survival. Fewer flowers meant fewer insects. The scrub moved in, hawthorn berries set foot and grew, birch flourished. The final stage, in many places, has been the arrival of the high woodland, in particular the beech and the yew. We are back to the Stone Age.

Far more damaging to the chalk grassland than non-farming has been the intensification of agriculture. Let us first look at the figures. The North Downs have 177,000 hectares of grass-covered chalk outcrop, of which a mere 902 hectares are actually unimproved chalk downland. The figures are from a 1966 survey — we can be sure matters are more serious now. These 902 hectares consist of 92 fragments, of which 83 are smaller than 20 hectares, parcels of land which farming, quarrying, urban development have been unable to reach. Much of the rest are places like Box Hill, Ranmore Common, parts of Hackhurst Downs, though even here the scrub is moving in fast. They have become museum pieces, to be visited, studied, admired certainly, but no longer simply enjoyed as part of the normal order of things.

What has happened to the downlands in the name of modern farming can be extended through most other parts of the British countryside. In the lifetime of most of us, agricultural prosperity meant an attractive, contained landscape, with small fields, hedgerows, hedge trees, copses, flanked by upland meadows grazed by sheep and cattle and safe from the plough. Now twin developments have changed all that. The first, a policy pursued by successive governments since the Second World War of trying to make Britain more self-sufficient in foodstuffs. Secondly, to achieve this end, agricultural machinery both bigger and more versatile than ever.

The cornerstone of this policy is price-support, by which farmers are guaranteed a minimum price for their produce, no matter how much of it they produce. It is often worthwhile, even essential, to exploit every nook and cranny of the farm. A helpful system of capital grants is available — for field drainage, hedge removal, hill ploughing and other 'improvement' schemes. Coupled with these incentives are sizeable tax concessions on the cost of machines and buildings as well as relief from local rates.

Martin

Kestrel

Skylark

Ox-eye daisy

Stoat

Six-spot
burnet moth

Birdsfoot trefoil

Field vole

Hairy violet

Wild strawberry

Cowslip

Common lizard

27

The character of farm buildings is changing too. No longer is grain stored in sacks in brick, stone or wooden barns, but instead in bulk in vertical iron silos, often taller than church spires. Financial and labour constraints demand that new buildings are roofed in corrugated asbestos, and not the tile or thatch that came from and melted into the landscape. Farmers are not obliged to regard as sacrosanct the 3,000 SSSIs (Sites of Special Scientific Interest), which should be sanctuaries for wildlife or geology designated by the Nature Conservancy Council.

This new industrial revolution has given us gargantuan combine harvesters, even bigger cultivators and spraying equipment, some with booms up to 15 metres wide shooting out chemical pesticide. Tractors climb the steep scarp and plough the land for cereal planting. Bigger machines demand bigger fields. Since the Second World War, a quarter of the hedgerows in England and Wales, well over 200,000 kilometres, have been grubbed out. The results are catastrophic for our flora and fauna. Where once good and prosperous farming spelt beauty and life to the countryside, now it often despoils and kills.

To try to reverse this trend, the Countryside Commission is working closely with farmers — in conjunction with bodies such as the Ministry of Agriculture, Fisheries and Food, the Nature Conservancy Council, the National Farmers Union etc. — to demonstrate that efficient, productive farming can co-exist with conservation and re-creation of the landscape and habitats. A number of 'demonstration farms' already illustrate how successful this co-existence can be.

Harrowing on the Downs

Farnham to Guildford

18 kilometres

Before setting out on our walk to the English Channel, we may wish to spend a few hours getting our bearings in one of England's more pleasant Georgian towns. Farnham first appeared in the history books in the seventh century, when the Wessex king, Caedwalla, presented it to the church. Another five centuries passed before the construction of its two most celebrated buildings. The castle, once a palace for the Bishop of Winchester, is surprisingly intact, despite damage in the Civil War and additions later. (Open daily from 2 pm.)

Outside the town, on the banks of the Wey, is Waverley Abbey, the first Cistercian monastery in England, and incidentally the inspiration for Walter Scott's Waverley novels. Today, only a clump of ruins evokes those far-away days.

Daniel Defoe, in his *Tour through the whole island of Great Britain*, recounts that after London, Farnham had the greatest corn market in the land, though he might have exaggerated when telling of 1,100 fully laden wagons delivering wheat on market day. Hop-growing also contributed to the town's well-being, though the last hop garden, in Crondall Road, disappeared in the mid-seventies. Today, fine red-brick and Georgian architecture, as in Castle, West and Downing Streets, testifies to an earlier prosperity.

Farnham's most famous son, the testy, outspoken, but also observant and indefatigable William Cobbett, whose *Rural Rides* provides a journalist's-eye view of early nineteenth-century England, would have been pleased to know that his town was at the beginning of a long journey, albeit on foot. We set off at the roundabout at the junction of the A31 and B3001, on the outskirts of the town close to the railway station. A finger-post, in neat green, announces *North Downs Way*.

Follow the A31 north-eastwards for a short while before bearing left into Darvills Lane. The noisy bypass draws slowly away. If still in need of reassurance about the direction, it is to be found at a house named *The Studio* with a modernistic torso statue in the garden. At the allotments, turn right along a stony track, reaching the River Wey at a

Farnham

Fishing in the River Wey, near Farnham

willow whose roots are so exposed that the tree might be doing an eastern elevation trick. Go through the white gate at Snayleslynch Farm, squeezed between rail and river, where fine willows line the bank.

Under the railway bridge at the kiln and suddenly we are in the country, with only accelerating motor-bikes intruding on views of cows and Georgian houses. The first stile of the morning replaces a foot-bridge marked on the old Ordnance Survey map and the remains of which can still be seen. Two more stiles and left along a tarred road again, left at the post box at Compton Lodge, crossing a bridge over the Wey, past Moor Park College, a converted manor house where, in 1696, Jonathan Swift penned *A Tale of a Tub.*

After this comes the first climblet of the day. At the top, as the metalled road curves to Moor Park Estate, watch out for the North Downs Way finger-post to the left next to a stile. It can be missed in summer foliage. The fence is to our right, but 50 metres on go through the squeeze stile, and now, with the fence on the left, there is a good view of Farnham. We proceed through more of these V-shaped stiles, into a copse with dead elms rocking in the wind, and a field where roe deer are sometimes browsing. They are, in certain seasons, the same rich red colour as the quarry to the left. Turn right up a bridleway, treading the leaf mould from the over-hanging beeches, then left, and left again at a house 200 metres on, quickly on to a tarred road, on to a path on the right which runs on to more tar, going right again, up to the Farnham golf club.

Left at the road junction by the clubhouse, harkening to cries of *Fore!* from the 18th and 19th holes, and then three minutes on, it is a relief to climb through a stile at the finger-post and walk along the grassy edge of the links. Nice spot for a sit-down. Cross a road on to a wide track and veer right soon after the acorn marker on the post. Then left along a flowery hedgerow, where the path has the air of having been walked for centuries. Indeed, I met a jolly couple falling about on their return journey from the local tavern.

Poppies push up through the golden barley, while in and next to the hawthorn hedge are field scabious, campion, yarrow, and the tiny heart-shaped seed-pods of the shepherd's purse. And the worts — St. John's, rag, pearl, and mug. Also to be found is the rarer Chinese mugwort, which can be burned as 'moxa', a heat treatment for gout or for stimulating acupuncture points. Wort, from the old English *wyrt*, a root.

Straight as a die towards Seale, a quiet hamlet where the loudest noise is from the wood-pigeon in the pines. At Landthorn Hatch Cottage, right on to the tar, and immediately left back into the pines, with oak saplings trying to break through the canopy. Signposts are clear, but can be overlooked in the summer greenery. Bear left, and 200 metres on, leftwards again across three stiles, and we come

The Hog's Back, from Seale

out facing the steep scarp of the Hog's Back. Up to now we have kept to the low ground, not yet on the downs, so that views are few and far between. The Hog's Back is a narrow ribbon of down's top, 16 kilometres by a half, whence ramblers have long been ousted by the A31 from Guildford to Farnham. We remain on the lower ground.

We continue eastwards towards Totford Hatch, where we cross the road and mount the gentle brown track to Puttenham Common, bearing left into a narrow path which seems to have been hewn out of the hillside. Beware nettles if in shorts or skirt. The extensive common is a Surrey County Council 'Open Space', good for strolls and scenic views.

The path leads into Lascombe Lane and so to Puttenham, a village of red-brick cottages and bumpy tiled roofs, converted stables and hop kilns, even a hop garden. Puttenham lies on the exact dividing line between chalk and sandstone, and materials from both geological strata are used in its buildings. Wind through the village, past the fort-like St. John the Baptist church, right at the main road and left opposite the Jolly Farmer. We pass the golf club, the bowling green, and eventually the Puttenham and Wanborough cricket pitch — matches Saturday and Sunday. Keep clear of the rifle range by going off the tar on to a stony road.

At Monkgrove Farm, fork left (the sign might be camouflaged in the hedge) and with more finger-posts, you are on Compton Heath, hazel trees and ivy enlacing the boles so heavily that the trees can be difficult to identify. Sinister when cloudy, light and dappled in the sun. The path goes under the A3 (note the crosses on the bridge parapets marking the Pilgrims' Way). Two minutes later, at Watt's Cottage, there is the chance to turn off into Compton, always a serious contender for the Surrey 'best kept village' cup. 'Bed and breakfast?' said a lady at the post office. 'It's not that sort of place' — though a householder did offer his field for a tent.

But Compton *is* friendly and, furthermore, boasts two of the gems of the walk, one precious, the other semi-precious. Under the Cedars of Lebanon, their cones in summer-time like white tulips, is the church of St. Nicholas, parts of which were there before William conquered. The balustrade screen to the upper sanctuary might be the oldest piece of wood in England, of oak or perhaps chestnut. It feels like bronze. The white pillars are of 'clunch' chalk, a once popular process of hardening the local limestone. The soft limestone came from a quarry of lower chalk only minutes away on the south side of the Hog's Back. Note the anchorite cell — but more of that when we get to Shere.

Semi-precious is the temple to the Victorian painter, George Frederick Watts, erected by his widow with the help of local craftsmen. Its style? Alhambra moorish, Byzantine, art nouveau, traces of Florentine and Pre-Raphaelite. You don't have to like it to be amazed.

Rejoin the Way, mounting a sunken sandy track, hedgerows coloured with dead nettle and cow parsley. Birds flutter, and to the left, the ever-faithful Hog's Back. Sandy Lane is then fringed by a wood of holly, beech and tangy pines. Through the trees to the right is Loseley House (see Gazetteer).

When the Way moves briefly on to tar, turn left on the gravel, and two minutes on, as the outskirts of Guildford appear, we follow the acorn sign along Piccard's Farm Road. It is uneventful, with rooks in the field, wood-pigeons in the trees, hazels laden with green nuts. On reaching the A3100, turn right (left goes into town) and, very soon, at The Ship, drop down over the rail bridge (Portsmouth-London) as the path falls sharply to the Wey for the third and last time. Out of school hours, lads fish for perch and chub. Since last

St Nicholas' church, Compton

33

encountered outside Farnham, the Wey has wound gently past Waverley's ruins, to Godalming and Shalford, 1½ kilometres to the south. A century and a quarter ago boats could reach the south coast along a 27-kilometre canal linking Shalford with Wisborough Green on the Arun. Today, like the railway which put it out of business, the canal, known as London's lost route to the sea, is disused and overgrown. (The railway track bed now forms part of the route for a new ramblers' *Downs Link* between the North and South Downs.)

There is as yet no bridge and the ferry is long gone, so short of hitching a lift with a passing pleasure cruiser, walk downstream along the tow path to the southern tip of Guildford.

Crossing a
'pinch' stile

Guildford to Box Hill

23 kilometres

Guildford is the county town of Surrey, seat of a modern cathedral, a new red-brick university, a medieval castle (close to our path) and a steep and ancient High Street (see Gazetteer). But we keep to the outskirts, cross the footbridge at the Jolly Farmer and walk back southwards (and up-stream) along the A281 road. As traffic whistles by, we console ourselves with the handsome sight of St. Catherine's Chapel, early fourteenth century, and now roofless, above the Wey.

Nearly one kilometre on, turn left into Pilgrims' Way, a residential street, joining at the spot where the North Downs Way will come when the river foot-bridge is built below St. Catherine's Hill. Towering limes line up as if awaiting inspection. Bear right through a gate and up into the fields.

Now the Way converges with the Pilgrims' Way for a time, though the two routes are different. For the most part, the medieval pilgrims took the low road to Canterbury. We take the high road. The tractor-marked path is hemmed in by barbed wire on each side. Chantries Woods are to the right, going up to Whinny Hill. There is a sign to the Chantries Youth Camping Site, run by Guildford Borough Council.

At the metalled road, follow the North Downs Way sign leftwards, then right through the oaks. Over the crest, with St. Martha's Priory Lodge to the right, go through the wooden bollards (coming the other way, take care to go through the oaks and not right on to the metalled road). Now comes the first real ascent of the walk, up the wide avenue leading to the lonely church on St. Martha's Hill (170 metres). Small wonder that John Bunyan, who once lived at Shalford, had the hill as his model for the Hill of Difficulty in *Pilgrim's Progress* (as the marshes of the Tillingbourne and Wey inspired the Slough of Despond). Built for endurance and not embellishment, the Norman-style St. Martha's was once parish church of Chilworth, over which it looks (now St. Thomas's is). There was a church on the hill in the twelfth century, but the present one was rebuilt from its ruins in the 1840s.

On the hill southwards are circular banks with external ditches, probably Early Bronze Age. Tradition also associates

River Wey, near Guildford

the rings with seventh-century Christian martyrs. Chilworth
was once renowned for the manufacture of gunpowder. From
the seat in front of St. Martha's look down into the Vale of the
Tillingbourne where the Tonbridge-bound railway was made
to take a wide curve in order to satisfy the Duke of
Northumberland, who objected to the smelly machine coming
too close to his mansion in Albury Park. Those were the days.

In misty weather a compass might be needed to take us
down the hill due east. Note the heather, a sign that we are,
for the moment, on lower greensand and not on chalk. Keep
the pines to the left and just before the pillbox be sure to take
the more modest path leftwards. (The Pilgrims' Way carries
straight on.) The narrow bridleway descends to the road,
where the North Downs Way sign is sometimes hidden in
trees to the left, next to Ramshackle Cottage. Beware of
nettles on the overgrown track, which adjoins the road.

And so to Albury Downs where Guildford people and their
dogs dot the landscape as in a Lowry canvas. At last the
widespread grassland gives us the feeling of being on real
downs. It is worth leaving the path for a brief sortie into the
woods. From the white under their oval leaves the
whitebeam look like flowering trees. We come out at
Newlands Corner car park, where refreshments are on offer.

Newlands Corner has a long and wide panorama over
Surrey and the Weald. On a clear day you can see, well not
for ever, but to the South Downs at Chanctonbury Rings, as
well as to Blackdown and Hindhead. The road leads north, off
the Way, to Clandon Park (see Gazetteer). Cross the A25
with care, and enter the woods south of the tea-room. There
are no views now, and the path is muddy, with chalk deeper
down under the clay cover. In fact, the next 11 or 12
kilometres to Ranmore Common are one of the best-
preserved stretches of natural chalkland in Surrey. Almost
without break it is Surrey County Council 'Open Space', with
scenic views from both on and off our path.

Wild raspberries edge this ancient drove road. To the right is West Hanger (*hanger* for a wood on the side of a steep hill). Two and a half kilometres on, the path runs into West Hanger car park. It crosses the road through the gate and becomes a narrow track sometimes muddied by horses, mopeds and rain. Moments after reaching a cemented dew pond, turn right along the tarred road and 30 metres on, left through what was once a gate, to Hollister Farm. Local historians believe this to be the site of a brothel frequented by that injudicious monarch King John. Bear left at what is today a farm, entering the woods through a gate. Five minutes later, a right fork leads to Netley House and the village of Shere, off the Way.

A visit to Shere — one of the prime picture postcard villages in Surrey — is well worthwhile. The one-kilometre descent is by London Lane, which headed towards the Thames before ever London was called *Londinium*. Shere has 'olde worlde' timber-framed pubs and houses, a Victorian well-head in a grotto, the Early English church of St. James, with a fine shingle spire almost as good as the one at Compton. Here, in the sunless north side, is the cell where, one August day in 1329, the anchoress, Christine, daughter of William the Carpenter, was walled up in the service of God. Granting her permission, the Bishop of Winchester wrote that she 'desires for the fulfilment of a better life to remove herself and spend her life in the service of God and in

St Martha's church, near Chilworth

The picturesque village of Shere

all sanctity and chastity in the churchyard of the parish church of Schire, striving with her whole heart to endure henceforth perpetual enclosure'.

Christine received her food through a grating, and watched the priest at the altar through the aptly named 'squint'. But she found her solitude so unbearable that she gave up, risking excommunication, only to apply for permission to go back to her sacred hide-out. Did she return of her own free will? Seven centuries later we still don't know.

Back on the downs, the road turns to tar, a relic of the days during the Second World War when the Canadian army, stationed in the area, set up a line of defence in case of a German landing. The pillboxes which proliferate in the woods are not marked on the map. Apparently they were so solidly constructed that it was too expensive to take them down.

Keep straight on the drove road, passing a disused water storage tank between two wide tracks coming up from the north side of the downs. More fine views across the Weald. A bench. . . . The name Abinger Hammer, the hamlet below, is a reminder of the iron-smelting industry which once flourished in the timber-rich weald and made a considerable contribution to the ships of the British navy. Hammer ponds are a feature of the Vale of Tillingbourne.

At a loop in the road, the Way drops into Hackhurst Downs. About 200 metres on, at the first fork, go left, reaching a rustic cross-roads with another bench. There are several paths here, so don't worry if you lose the Way as long as altitude is maintained. The path then becomes a well-worn walk through grass and then trees. It falls to another clearing, dropping right and crossing another path, before going slightly downhill to reach an obvious track in the trees. There are acorns and pillboxes and we end up on the road. (Coming the other way, the route is moré exactly marked.) Down the tar it is four kilometres to Holmbury St. Mary youth hostel, with Ewhurst Green hostel another five kilometres on.

Climb the busy road for 200 metres, stepping back into the downs at the North Downs Way sign. Beyond another pillbox an acorn indicates the Way is not up, but along, skirting White Downs. Pickett's Hole is an area of ancient woodland, but the downs themselves, once chalk grassland, are now mostly scrub, with birch taking over. Before long, beech trees, and yews on the steeper slopes, will be the dominant vegetation. But since April 1981, eight kilometres from eastern Hackhurst Downs through White Downs to the Denbies (Ranmore Common) have been under National Trust management so we can look forward to grassland restoration. The path narrows. Boots may trip on roots if we are distracted by aircraft flying in and out of Gatwick Airport.

Dorking appears out of the summer haze (or winter mist). Who says Surrey isn't pastoral? Then steeply up White Downs (again a pillbox) bearing right, directed by occasional yellow arrows painted on trees. The beeches creak in the breeze. On one is carved the name of 'E. A. Well 1940',

Dorking, from Ranmore Common

Dark green fritillary   Silver-spotted skippers

perhaps a Canadian soldier whiling away the fruitless hours. Other inscriptions are more like hieroglyphics on stones in the desert. A first set of gates not quite in the kissing style, and then another, and just off the Way there is a patch of grass reached over a stile from where Dorking can be viewed over lunch. Westcott village, lying between the chalk downs and the sandstone Surrey Hills, which here almost touch each other, is at our feet.

Beyond The Spains, a path leads off left to the Tanners Hatch youth hostel 1½ kilometres away in the Polesden Lacey estate (see Gazetteer). The path runs arrow-like into Ranmore Common, where Dorking children fly kites and mothers perambulate. Bear right, with the church steeple in vision, climb two stiles along the fence, leading out on to the metalled road. To the left is the main part of Ranmore Common, now National Trust owned. On the chalk grassland of the escarpment below us flutter 42 of the 56 species of butterfly regularly spotted in this country. One of these is a Surrey speciality, the silver-spotted skipper, while in August and September we may see the lovely Adonis blue on the wing.

The Way goes past the house called The Old Post Office (a

Marbled white   Green hair-streak

bus stop here to Dorking), and the church of St. Barnabas, sub-titled 'The Church of the North Downs Way' Barnabas, the 'son of consolation', has no link with walking. But the vicar says walkers are especially welcome. We join the bridleway on the right (marked to Dorking) which slips along between wire fences. Soon we are at the nearest point to the town, with towering behemoths of trees almost at arm's length. Surprised rabbits scamper from under our feet. The road is hard on the soles. We skirt the downs, sometimes going north in Ashcombe Wood.

Box Hill's chalky cheeks approach. Descend at the acorn, then under the mournful Victorian railway bridge, coming out at the biggest hazard of the Way so far, the A24 dual carriageway linking Leatherhead and Dorking (this, too, is Stane Street, the Roman road to Chichester). For safety, follow the road for half a kilometre to cross via the subway.

Otherwise, wait patiently to cross, stopping on the island for a good look left. We have negotiated the Mole Gap. There is a choice of ways to cross the river. The foot-bridge, slightly to the north, is near to Flint Cottage, where the novelist George Meredith lived for 40 years (now owned by the National Trust, but no visits). Nearby, in the Burford Bridge

St Barnabas' church, Ranmore Common

Hotel, John Keats put the finishing touches to *Endymion*.

A sign warning that the stepping-stones are dangerous leads us to the alternative crossing. Indeed, some of the 18 stones are upturned or under water. In heavy rain it takes about two days for the rivulets to come down to make the Mole dangerous for a stones crossing. But wading through with bare feet on a glancing summer's day is a refreshment not to be missed.

The origin of the name is still a matter for controversy, but it could justly be attributed to its animal counterpart. For over the centuries, the Mole has burrowed through the chalk, first undermining, then flattening out the downs. Myths abound about gigantic swallow-holes, through which sizeable objects, even tree trunks, have disappeared, to resurface downstream after much meandering through the subterranean limestone.

The right bank is a friendly place, with Dorking and Leatherhead mums watching their kids paddling or swinging Tarzan-like from the trees over the water.

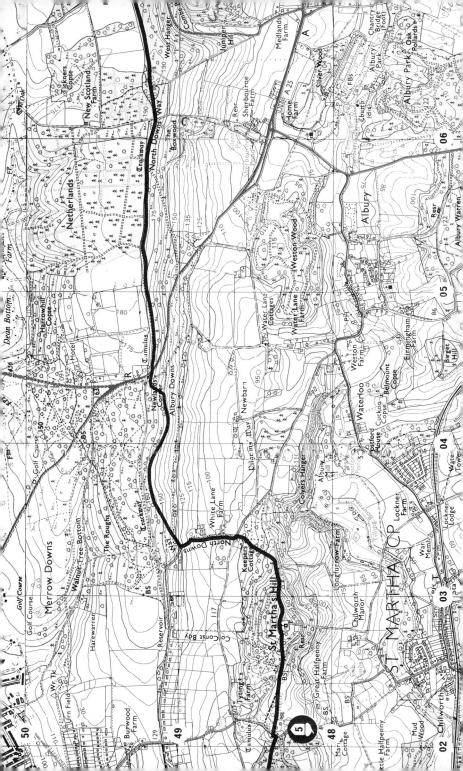

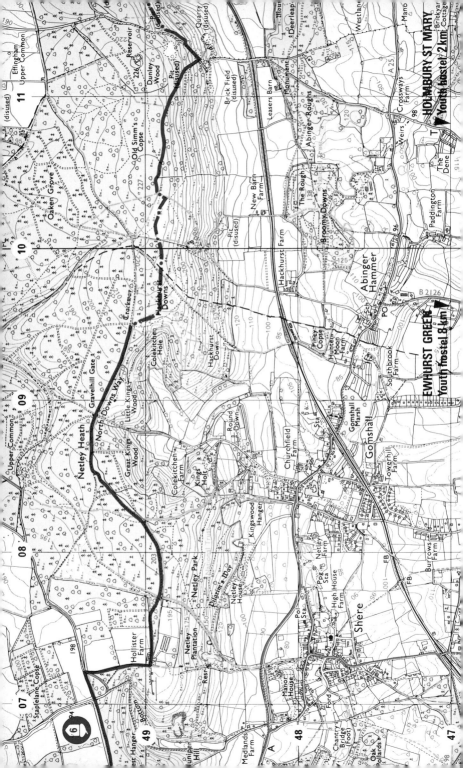

Box Hill to Oxted

26½ kilometres

And so the slog up Box Hill, starting alongside an intricate lacework of exposed beech roots. The urge to sightsee recedes in direct proportion to the steepness of the ascent. After the long walk on top of the downs, thoughts move from feet to lungs. It is folly to take a wrong turning. Follow the path scrupulously, helped by acorn signs, moving gradually to the right, up and along the terraced steps.

Long ago, the box tree escaped from its domestic confines and found a home in this limestone hill to which it gives its name. The tree is sparser than it once was, due to large-scale fellings for wood engravings in the eighteenth century. The box tree takes 40 years to mature and is not a good commercial proposition.

After anything from five to 20 minutes the path levels out, reaching the monument (171 metres) to Leopold Salomons of Norbury Park 'who gave Box Hill to the nation, 1914'. The wide sweep of the Weald stretches to the Devil's Dyke and the Chanctonbury Rings 40 kilometres away on the South Downs ... if the weather is kind. Aircraft move about ceaselessly over Gatwick Airport.

Take good care here, for acorn signs on stakes are sometimes twisted round or removed by vandals. I also found some cheeky 12-year-old lads round a fire in an especially inflammable part of the woods. My stern warning to extinguish immediately was met with four-letter abuse. Box Hill, one of Surrey's most trampled beauty spots, is struggling to survive.

The gravel path is the Way, and we bear left when it becomes a grass track. The path reappears higher up in the trees, crossing a broad, then a narrow, track. Several well-marked turns and we mount steps to the left, going right at the top, reaching a hairpin bend, resisting the temptation to drop down, and instead, going over the bend and down more steps. Yet more steps follow. Off the Way is a vantage point with a fine view over the Betchworth Hills, where the chalk flesh of the downs is dramatically exposed in the disused Brockham quarry, now acquired by the Surrey County Council. The quarry and lime kilns are not forbidden to the public, but the descent from the path is dangerous.

The climb up Box Hill

. . . and the view from the top

Before Box Hill village (which is not seen from the path) follow the acorn to the right, treading potato crisp packets, empty beer cans and dumped cardboard boxes below the caravan park. There are yews about, though not the original ones that preceded man's arrival on the downs. Here, too, is a memorial to 'Quick, an English thoroughbred — 26/9/36 — 22/10/44', a short but no doubt happy life. Descend through the hawthorn, along what is known as the 'Red Road', winding along the chalky path. Then past a lime kiln (part of the Betchworth workings), and an incongruous avenue of buddleia — a favourite haunt of butterflies. Once alongside the quarry, watch out for the turn off to the right, past a handsome kiln, its 18-metre tower of brick almost topped by creepers. Over a brick viaduct, more buddleia.Once again we join the low-lying Pilgrims' Way on the metalled road a half a kilometre from Betchworth railway station. At Brockham, the museum trust restores old industrial machinery, including trains and locomotives. Occasional open days.

On reaching the road we turn left by the post box and carry on up the road which leads to Pebble Coombe. The 'Reduce speed now' warning does not apply to walkers. Cranmer Cottage (right) looks Tudor, but is in fact of 1929 vintage, as is evident from the over-large windows. The timbers are said to come from Archbishop Cranmer's palace. At the North Downs Way finger-post the path leads off right towards the downs, which appear through the beech trees on the far left.

Over a stile and through a gate which is, believe it or not, the first gate we have actually opened and shut on the walk so far. Note the warning about dogs on leashes. There were (in August) cows in the field, but in the lambing season no doubt sheep as well. Farmers are entitled by law to shoot dogs they find worrying their livestock.

The Way rises through clumps of bright flowers visited by bees and flirted with by butterflies. Our route is well marked as it skirts the hill, passing a disused lime pit. Follow the finger-post to the left up a narrow, overgrown path which runs out on to a grass track. Along the slope of Buckland Hills there are pretty views of the Weald, accompanied by the ubiquitous air traffic.

Duck under the logs, remembering to take your pack with you. These barriers are to discourage horse folk, who have a bridleway at the top of the hill. At the foot of Juniper Hill, look back to see the Betchworth quarry across the wide loop of fields. Now follows a pleasant walk along the bottom of Juniper Hill until reaching the turn-off up Colley Hill. Either an ancient drove road or a river-bed, the hill is damp in summer, and a paddy field in the autumn rains. Signs of horses' hooves, which encourage ankle-bending unevenness. The hill turns back on itself, going north-west for a while. Note the fine-needled yews. The path is enclosed by wire fences, but listen to the birds' song, rather, as you sweat it out through the clicking contour lines.

The South Downs from Box Hill

A wooden fence heralds our arrival on the hill-top, and after two right turns (note the post marking the boundary for tolls on coal entering London) re-enter the woods. There are several paths, but be sure to maintain height, heading along the grassy verge, seizing the opportunity to rest on the welcoming seat. On a hot summer's day, with trees in full leaf, the buildings in the nearby town of Reigate barely stand out from the landscape. Colley Hill is National Trust property, and much loved by the citizens of Reigate for sandwich lunches and dog-walking.

Work your way above The Saddle Knob and The Horseshoe, heading for a temple-like edifice, presented to the borough of Reigate in 1909 by Lieutenant-Colonel Robert William Inglis 'for the benefit of the public'. The mosaic

London from Reigate Hill

drinking basin no longer provides liquid refreshment, so that now the temple serves simply as a landmark to walkers and a shelter from inclement weather. Behind the temple the acorn points along a road covered by chestnut and beech. Through the gates at a National Trust sign for Reigate Hill (230 metres) next to the East Surrey Water Company tower (AD 1924), soon the town of Banstead is visible to the north-east. And further on, there is a salutary reminder of the nearness of London as the National Westminster building in the City comes clearly into view, some 40 kilometres away. Other landmarks are the Post Office Tower and the square Euston Tower.

And southwards, the natural landmarks of Ditchling Beacon (248 metres) some 40 kilometres to the South Downs

The 'temple', Reigate Hill

Way. At another National Trust sign for Reigate Hill is a plea to avoid littering, lighting fires and damaging trees or plants.

The iron foot-bridge spans the Old Brighton Road, the A217, to a kiosk café, open every day except Christmas. (A 15-minute walk from here to Reigate town, and there are regular buses.)

Along Wingate Hill, the lake at Gatton Park is seen deliciously through the old yew and beech. Merstham, our next port of call, is beyond.

The path almost touches the road before running into a tarred drive on the side of a greenhouse at Stonehouse, No. 2 Tower Lodge Cottages. The Way winds past new buildings of the Royal Alexandra and Albert School, a children's boarding establishment. This is Gatton Park, once a rotten borough, which in the days before the 1832 Reform Act returned two MPs to the House of Commons from a local population drawn from 23 houses. The 'elections' took place in the little town hall. The church of St. Andrew, which has relics brought back from Lord Monson's grand tour, is locked up. The estate was later owned by the Colman mustard family. Turn left at the giant cedars in front of the chapel-cum-assembly hall, and at the end of the avenue of yellow haws and red-berried thorn trees, go out of the grounds at a thatched lodge with a fine weeping ash.

Ten minutes on, follow the sign to Orpington Nurseries and soon the path goes through a mildewed gate, a kissing gate and stile, and with Gatton Bottom to the left, the roofs of the quarrying village of Merstham appear through the cornheads. This is an excellent example of a well-used right of way through a field. Do not wander off for a snooze in the field. You may not be seen again till the combine harvester appears. The village cricket ground looms (in winter it is the

Old Reigation hockey field). The stile at deep long on leads to Quality Street, Merstham. It is indeed a street of quality, but the reason for its name is that the actors Sir Seymour Hicks and Ellen Terry lived in the fifteenth-century Old Forge house while playing in James Barrie's play, *Quality Street.*

Walk left up Quality Street, away from the bustle of (another) London to Brighton road, the A230. At Merstham House, the lane leads off next to a building with crooked timbers (number 312 of Surrey County Council's buildings of special interest). A modern foot-bridge crosses the new M25. Speeding traffic can be a dizzying experience to the airborne pedestrian above, so watch out for vertigo. Right at the rectory gate, over the A23, to Rockshaw Road, and then above two railway lines, both on the London to Brighton line, though only the first goes through Merstham station. Opened in 1841, it was the first rail link between the capital and the south coast.

Now follows a long hike along the unyielding pavement of Rockshaw Road, which has substantial houses, cultivated gardens and tidy lawns. Soles throb and at last, at a bungalow, the finger points across the field, which leads under the motorway and up Ockley Hill.

The solid climb is along a well-trodden path through fields. At the top are views of Redhill, and northwards, London and again the bank skyscraper. A cement beacon marks the hill at 662 feet (202 metres). A few hundred metres on, North Downs Way and Pilgrims' Way signs point along a stony road. Off the tree-shaded walk is a sign 'Caterham District Scouts camping ground — private'.

At Willey Park Farm, go through the gate and straight on, and not between the farm buildings. A small, round flint tower beside a pool could be a pilgrims' amenity — or a rich man's folly.

Petrified weeping tree, Arthur's Seat

Before descending War Coppice Road, note a (real) folly in the field and a petrified weeping tree. Here, too, is Arthur's Seat, an earthwork which may or, more likely, may not, have Round Table associations. The metalled road is cool in the sun (or protected from the drizzle) under the trees. War Coppice Garden Village has a prosperous, manicured air about it. An amiable trackway runs off from a stile at Hextall's Lane, skirting the hill with fine views of Bletchingley (from just off the Way). Humming and whining from the M25 creep back closer to us.

At Gravelly Hill vantage point, Godstone appears. With binoculars, the chauvinistic walker can count the number of British cars on the motorway. A seat is here, and a generously placed tap, with cold water for drinking or slopping down a sticky shirt. Children risk their necks and the seats of their pants to slide down the chalk path careering off the verge at a gradient of about two in three.

On towards yet another London radial road, the A22 to Eastbourne. To get there, leave Gravelly Hill by the acorn finger — which now replaces the North Downs Way finger — along the bridleway. We drop through the woods, then swing left on a hoof-churned path, through ragged vegetation. The footpath leading off the Way at Fosterdown to Godstone avoids the busy road. On reaching the tar, be sure to turn off right opposite the gipsy camp, along a slightly hidden path which crosses the A22 road bridge and then moves quickly back into the countryside above a disused quarry. The Way twists and turns a fair bit, crossing a field, then right on to a stony track, soon bearing left through gates at the North Downs Way sign, curving through a field ablaze with willow-herb, ragwort, teasel, honeysuckle, all wooed by cooing wood-pigeons, and buzzing bees.

Down some steps we go across a metalled road on to a public footpath up to a road where it is right on to cement strips, up Winders Hill, along a hedged road (note the fine beech hedge).

The tarred road is a convenient turn-off to Godstone, which, helped by ponds, has managed to retain its village green atmosphere in the face of a ceaseless stream of motor traffic. The White Hart is one of the most celebrated pubs in the county, with genuine beams, wooden doors and unexpected steps testifying to its sixteenth-century vintage. Philosophers among ramblers may wish to pay tribute at the churchyard grave of S. F. Taylor, the father of rambling, who died in 1908.

There are air shafts about from the disused quarries. They are 20 metres deep, dangerous and should be left alone, just as the disused quarries are there to be ignored by everyone but pot-holers. Watch out for adders in the spring basking on the edge of the scrub, too dozy from post-hibernation awakening to scuttle away. By the summer they are friskier and less frequently seen. Coloured yellow to brown to black with diamond markings on the back, they are rarely longer than 80 centimetres.

So, go over the stile and across a busy road and climb to a clearing in the hawthorn with views over Godstone. The way up to Tandridge Hill is at times uneven, with roots stubbing at the toes, or terribly muddy when enclosed between barbed wire. The last stretch is an overgrown path just above the road (most ramblers seem to prefer the road). The acorns come as confirmation, and eventually the path rejoins the road at the top of Tandridge Hill. From the hill-top, bear right off the road along a clear path, not wandering too far from the tar. After rain it is mud, mud, glorious mud. Some 500 metres later we run into a North Downs Way post just before a house (seats along here from which to spy on Oxted and Limpsfield) and then descend 85 steps at South Hawke, restrained from plunging into the fields below by a handrail. Directly underneath us is the tunnel of the Oxted to Purley railway.

The contour runs in and out of the thicket, then down at an acorn post to a wheatfield, in the midst of which an incongruous finger-post directs us leftwards. Make for the next North Downs Way sign on the edge of the wood, and then to another marker on the right of the row of houses leading down from the quarry.

From here we can make a diversion along Chalkpit Lane to Oxted, passing under the motorway which has restored the village's Tudor High Street to a haven of security. Accommodation here, and in adjacent Limpsfield, where music lovers will find Delius buried in the Norman church.

Limpsfield church

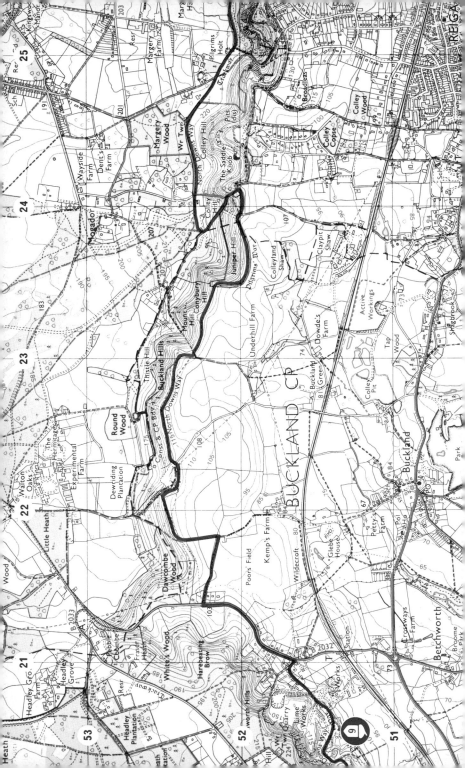

Titsey Place from Betsom's Hill

Chevening House

Oxted to Otford

20½ kilometres

To begin the day which will take us out of Surrey and into Kent we plunge up the stairs in the hedge, keeping next to the fence, with the motorway still uncomfortably close by. Beyond, accompanying us from Dorking, runs the Vale of Holmesdale. We get some idea of the marvellous trees in the Titsey Plantation, while at our feet is a busy wild flower world — poppies, teasels, speedwell (which sped the pilgrims on their way), and the little scarlet pimpernel, a survivor of the holocaust of herbicides which has destroyed so many old field favourites.

Stile succeeds stile, until steps go down and then left, for the one-kilometre climb up Botley Hill, a pleasant path untouched by tyre or hoof marks. The 'summit' (267 metres) is the highest point on the North Downs Way, but the trees obscure any thoughts of a view. East again from here, avoiding the stubby roots along the High Trees path which parallels the road. Nearly one kilometre on, the acorn heralds a short, sharp spurt, to a path with a welcome bench and even a table for picnicking, or perhaps a game of chess. Views of the Kent Weald and below, Titsey Place lake. Nearby are the remains of a Romano-British temple and a Roman villa, both excavated in the last century.

The Way continues over stiles and through a wheatfield to Clarks Lane Farm. Here, instead of climbing the stile, keep in the field with the fence to the left, avoiding a minor pond formed from a tap and used by cows. More stiles, before log steps climb to the road, the idyllic Pilgrims Farm in the valley below. The B2024 runs south to Quebec House, Westerham (see Gazetteer). The North Downs Way runs under the trees (beware falling conkers in autumn) into a Surrey County Council 'Open Space', Hill Park, Tatsfield.

One kilometre on, at a gate marked 'Private Road' (but public for walkers), the Way crosses the frontier of Surrey into the mighty county of Kent. The traveller may wish to sit down on the concrete seat for a celebratory sip of cow's milk. Here, on Betsom's Hill, is the highest point on the Kent side of the journey.

Kent seems hardly different from Surrey, except that now our guide is a concrete signstone, adorned with 'North Downs'

Way', acorn and directional arrow. One defect of Kent signposting, however, is that the inscriptions, like those in churchyards, are liable to weather and become illegible. But the concrete is difficult to vandalise, let alone to remove altogether, for souvenir or other nefarious purpose.

One and a half kilometres on, the road runs into the A233, where the waymark might in high summer be hidden in the long grass. South down the A233 it is 1½ kilometres to the village of Westerham, with Winston Churchill's home, Chartwell, three kilometres farther on (see Gazetteer). But we climb up the road, soon turning off right. The Way curves around a wheatfield, there are darting birds and a sweet-scented grove and a warning 'Private shoot — keep to footpath'. The stile leading left uphill is in the hedge. At the top of the contour, where inevitably the panting walker pauses for breath, refreshment or lunch, there is a view of Chevening House.

The estate was bequeathed to the nation by Earl Stanhope when he died without heirs in 1957. The house, its fine park and tree-fringed lake, were put at the disposal of Prince Charles, but he has since given them up. They are now to be used by the Foreign Secretary of the day. The house is almost certainly the design of the seventeenth-century architect, Inigo Jones. Chevening is not open to the public, which is unfortunate, for it contains such historic relics as Prime Minister Pitt's dispatch-box and the telescope through which the Duke of Wellington watched the Battle of Waterloo.

A hundred metres from the vantage point, the Way leads from a stile along the top of a wide and lengthy field. When I walked here in the summer of 1980 a bull was grazing, or more exactly, resting — waiting? — on our very North Downs Way. Now this is not illegal. In a dozen English and Welsh counties including Kent (but not Surrey) bylaws have allowed bulls to be pastured in fields with rights of way, provided cows or heifers were present. The 1981 Wildlife and Countryside Act has since changed the law to permit beef and cross-breed bulls, but not the allegedly more malevolent dairy bulls, to pasture in fields in all English and Welsh counties. So the downs walker should take care in Surrey now as well.

The stile takes us out of the field. Another warning of private shooting. This is wild border country. Indeed, for nearly a kilometre we walk along the dividing line between Greater London and Kent. Round a cornfield and the Way is fringed with creeping thistle, barbed wire and hawthorn. More stiles cut in and out of the fields. The motorway can now, like a good child, be seen and not heard. The path falls gently between hedgerows. Watch out for an acorn stile hidden to the left. The route cuts across and round fields occupied by cows dressed in yellow collars. The arrows on the concrete waymarks should be carefully observed to see whether they point onwards or sideways. At the road on

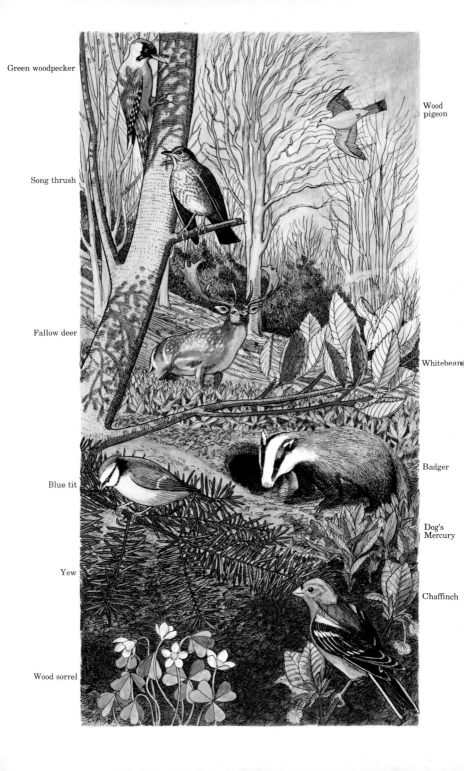

Green woodpecker

Wood pigeon

Song thrush

Fallow deer

Whitebeam

Badger

Blue tit

Dog's Mercury

Yew

Chaffinch

Wood sorrel

Hogtrough Hill turn left on to a path next to the tar, going through a T-junction, and at Stoneings Farm back into the fields, alongside the road. This is rough walking on a knobbly path, with dull vistas about. In time, as the North Downs Way gains in popularity, these new or long unused paths, often negotiated with farmers to take us off the tar, will be smoother going.

Before running on to the metalled road again, the North Downs Way passes close to Knockholt Beeches, which, at 237 metres above sea-level, is a prominent local landmark. From the Sundridge road it is a short walk to the village, with its wireless telegraph station, pub and, in St. Katherine's churchyard, a yew which might have been there before the Tudors ascended the throne of England. Emmetts Garden, beyond Sundridge (Gazetteer) is diverted to from here. But the Way turns off the road before the village, coursing around fields where cows and horses nibble. It is easy to follow. Suddenly, as we climb a stile, there is an arresting keyhole of Chevening House through an avenue of trees. Soon, over a stile under an ash, we go straight over the road following the sign to Otford, and not down the hill to Chevening. The established path follows the wheatfields. It rises towards, but does not meet, the A21 Sevenoaks bypass.

Descend a clear path across a vast meadow; rabbits are about, as well as mushrooms or maybe toadstools. Ideal to pause here for a picnic or a sip of barley-water while contemplating the splendid Darent Valley and Sevenoaks beyond. The path runs alongside a thorn hedge, coming out at an acorn sign barely discernible in the nettle and thistle. Once more it drops, and over a stile we go, with some relief on to the road. Now walk as quickly as possible along the pavement parallel to the bypass, crossing it after less than a kilometre, and the same distance farther on is the Rose and Crown at Dunton Green. A sharp left at the pub, past a milestone (London 21, Sevenoaks 3), and then right, before the higgledy-piggledy roof and beams of Donnington Manor, along a waymarked lane. Admire the downs from below.

It is about here that a section of the M25 London orbital motorway from the Sevenoaks bypass to Swanley is planned to run north up the Darent Valley. Environmental groups, the Ramblers' Association and the Countryside Commission among them, have mounted sturdy opposition to what they see as the desecration of a lovely valley.

Over the Sevenoaks-London railway line, and we enter suburbia — houses with little gardens, a revving lawn-mower, dogs at your ankles, the six o'clock news, mopeds, pussies waiting to be let in, weeping willows — indeed, it is Willow Park.

The path rejoins the Pilgrims' Way, where we turn right, crosses the Darent, thence along Otford's main street up to the railway station. Frequent connections to Sevenoaks, and the other way to London-Blackfriars, Holborn and Victoria.

Knockholt
Beeches

Down the A225 to Knole House (see Gazetteer). Otford's strategic position on the river made it a pretty important place in olden times. Thomas à Becket lived here, but his house is gone. The remains of the Archbishop of Canterbury's palace are close by the village green and pond. Henry VIII bedded here on his way to the Field of the Cloth of Gold.

Lepiota mastoida   Roman snail   St George's mushroom

Otford to Medway Bridge M2 (West)

23¾ kilometres

Up from Otford station, the North Downs Way turns right at the first crossroads, and soon up a brick path which rises briskly between well-kept gardens to Otford Mount. So without much ado, there is a clearing of the lungs for the day's proceedings. A warning to keep dogs on a leash. A tumulus, or barrow, an ancient sepulchral mound, is a reminder of the New Stone Age people who, 5,000 years ago, settled valleys like the Darent. These were Britain's first farmers, who cleared the land and planted barley and wheat.

Before entering the thicket, look back at the village and picture the pilgrims, perhaps Geoffrey Chaucer among them, winding through the valley. The walking here is peaceful beneath the faithful beech. The stakes and stiles have a yellow way indicator, vivid enough not to be missed. A stone in a meadow gives the altitude as 669 feet (204 metres).

We follow the tarred Rowdow Lane, but very soon it is back into the fields, working around the fringes through stiles low enough for young horses to jump. At the gates leading to Hildenborough Hall, take the right-hand path outside the wire, to drop down to a seat with views of the verdant Weald. A path descends to the Kemsing youth hostel. The crinkle-crankle wall in Kemsing churchyard is worth a minor detour.

From here a series of well-trodden paths could confuse, but keep east and high, watching carefully for a sunken lane that climbs due north to Hildenborough Hall, now a Christian conference centre. Needless to say, it is a friendly place, with residents ready to point out the right direction. If none is about, follow the signs eastwards, keeping close to the hill's edge. From Kester it is a short and rewarding diversion to the Rising Sun pub at Ashdown Farm. Beyond Kester, the tar is quickly rejoined, turning left. After a short distance, leave the road on the right after Cotman's Ash, moving through a succession of small fields, each with the exit stiles or gates visible at the far side. Beyond Summeryards Wood the trackway is resumed and we pass under an altar of giant beeches before crossing the metalled road to Kemsing. Down briefly, cross the stile on the left and descend, resisting the temptation to gallop unceremoniously to the next stile (coming the other way, aim for the higher patch of exposed

75

earth). The gate is 300 metres across the field. It is your right of way, so head straight and true for the exit.

The waymark, in summer at least, may be lost in the nettles, but our route is indisputably east along the green lane, a three-kilometre stroll into Wrotham (pronounced 'Rootham'). Comfortable walking it is, as the wheat sings in the wind, and birds wheel. Here flourishes the nettle-leafed bellflower, one of nature's great opportunists, which has climbed on the bandwagon of fear generated by the real stinging nettle (no relation) by developing similar-looking leaves. Which do not sting.

We have dropped altitude and for the first time in Kent an apple orchard runs alongside. Abruptly, at Blacksole Field, we run into Wrotham. Turn right at Pilgrims' Cottage for a diversionary call at the village (and the Three Post Boys). Remains behind the church of yet another archbishop's palace — most of the materials were cannibalised in Edward III's day for the 'new' palace at Maidstone. The clock in the church tower is nearly 400 years old. Across the square, in Wrotham Place, the egregious Henry VIII waited for confirmation that Anne Boleyn had been beheaded.

The quiet of Wrotham vanishes over the M20, London's chief outlet to the south-east coast. The M26 runs just south of the village, with the motorways converging a couple of kilometres to the east, so that Wrotham is locked into two sides of a triangular nightmare. Negotiate the bridge and continue along a road between fields, still called Pilgrims' Way, though it is by no means certain that they came this way to Canterbury. Until the route has been fully established in this section, we follow the Pilgrims' Way from a house called (appropriately) 'Chaucers', before entering

Apple orchard, near Wrotham

Blackbird

Little owl

Lapwing

Mistle thrush

Tree
sparrow

Hognore Wood a kilometre or so on. All is sweet again. This is another of the North Downs Way's hearty climbs, but it is cool under the ceiling of ancient boughs. At the top (altitude 209 metres) is a waterhole and a wall that once formed part of the kitchen garden of the Waterlow estate, much of which was dismantled in 1933. The house on the left was the gardener's cottage.

Right at the Vigo Inn, then left into the woods just before the overhead bridge and we are in Trosley Country Park (though the parish itself is the unshortened 'Trottiscliffe'), a popular walking spot for local villagers. In the car park, an information centre has leaflets on waymarked walks. But we ignore the lead-off paths and recommended rambles and stick to the wider way along the softness of yew needles. Cooing doves, wind in leaves, young lovers hand in hand, whooping schoolboys up to minor mischiefs. Two to three kilometres along, through Downs Wood and Great Wood, there is a short climb leftwards, a kissing gate, a hairpin bend and a muddy descent through the contours of what was no doubt once a drove road. A notice that the path is *'Unsuitable for motors'*. We are back on the Pilgrims' Way.

But before moving on, we might wish to make a five-minute detour south to the megalithic burial chamber, Coldrum Long Barrow (National Trust). The massive sarsen stones are in place, but the remains of the people buried

The Medway from Holly Hill

there, perhaps 4,000 years ago, are on display at the nearby Trottiscliffe Church.

Back on the path, views of Kent come and go through the hazel and beech. A waymark at a pillbox confirms this to be the right direction. Approaching the Medway, the birdlife becomes more varied. All the year round there are the finches, blackbirds, song thrushes, mistle thrushes, tree sparrows. In May, the nightingale sings night and day. And from about the third week in April, the cuckoo is heard, only to fly away south in July. But rarer birds are about. The little owl, unlike other members of its family, is seen by day, perched on a fence post or in a tree, or in the autumn on a bale of hay, waiting for its snack of a careless mouse.

At another waymark, acorn and stile the North Downs Way turns left, heading north, which direction it will follow for the next eight kilometres or so, until the Medway is crossed. Ancient travellers would, in all likelihood, have carried on eastwards to ford the river at Snodland, or farther downstream at Cuxton.

We cross the cornfield, working right alongside the fence, and gradually, then breathlessly, move up on a grassy verge to Holly Hill Lodge, or to the vantage point below the road. Snodland is below, and another Medway valley village, Birling, left centre. Farther along on the metalled road, towards Holly Hill itself, the landscape changes dramatically — breathtaking views of the Medway bridge, the Channel, power stations, and beyond, on the far downs, the handsome cliff face of Blue Bell Hill.

When the tar turns to stone beyond Holly Hill Wood, and then bends, the Way goes straight along a narrow, sometimes sodden, track, wellnigh impassable in the rainy season except by hanging on to birch branches, or by transferring to

78

wellingtons. (A new path is being prepared at the time of writing.)

Half right, beyond Greatpark Wood, the Way passes two acorn stakes, goes under a pylon into the trees, then crosses a farm road where the waymark can be missed, thence along a narrow path next to a wooden shack in a chestnut grove. We see a large field where turnips may be thriving. The land hereabouts belongs to the Blue Circle Cement Company. Though one day it could be quarried, for the moment the fields are left to their own devices, untouched by high-powered agriculture. They are not sprayed with weed or insect killer, so that fairly rare flowers abound. Now, in August, a field of chicory, the seed of which fattens pheasants for the autumn shoot, is spattered with corn spurrey, rust red woundwort, teasels, red bartsia (same family as foxglove), and even corn sow thistles. In March, there are stinking hellebore in the woods around, violets and primroses in April, bee orchids in the late spring.

Through the woods and at an acorn on a post on the left-hand side, the arrow points to the right. After which, veer left into Wingate Wood. A disused chalk pit is unseen at the crest of the down. Unannounced, the North Downs Way dives left under the pylon to cornfields in Dean Valley (it was a hop field until recently — see oast-house at Dean Farm). The shooting sound does not herald the demise of a pheasant, but is an automatic birdscarer, released every few minutes when enough pressure builds up.

Wealden house at Upper Bush

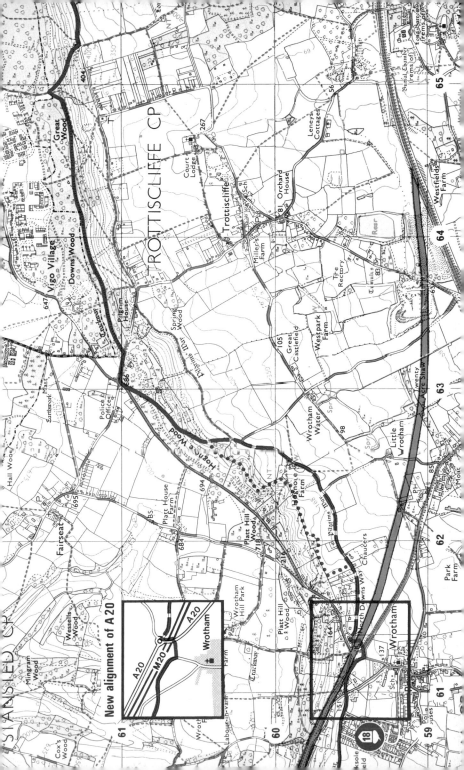

New alignment of A20

Medway Bridge
to Hollingbourne

23¾ kilometres

Almost 20 centuries ago, the Romans built their own M2, between *Dubris* and *Londinium,* crossing the Medway, a daunting natural barrier, at *Durobrivae* (Rochester). The road was later called Watling Street. Today's bridge, upstream from the city, 1½ kilometres long, starting back from the bank to avoid the marshy ground, is the major link between London and the Channel ports. A ceaseless flow of traffic is guaranteed to keep the rambler company. In mid-bridge there is a feeling of being suspended in mid-air, like the hovering kestrel which is attracted to these modern contraptions.

Upstream are factory chimneys, bobbing yachts, tractors, an almost Victorian air. The beyond, which we cannot see, is the rural river, fringed by hop fields and apple orchards, meandering from its Sussex source near East Grinstead, past Tonbridge, Twyford and the county town, Maidstone. Downstream is the conurbation of (from the left) Strood, Rochester, Chatham and Gillingham (see Gazetteer).

We leave the bridge at Borstal, where the prison has given its name to the countrywide system of juvenile reformative institutions. The Way turns south, leading through Nashenden Farm yard with its oast-houses, up past a tumulus on the left, Shoulder of Mutton Wood and Nine Acre Wood, on to Wouldham Down, the comforting beech at our side — and a barbed wire fence.

On the far bank of the Medway the route recently traversed stretches to Wrotham and beyond. Closer to us, in Wouldham church, lies Walter Burke, purser on the *Victory* at the Battle of Trafalgar, and in whose arms Admiral Nelson expired. Farther along is Snodland where 600 years ago grapes were grown. Today it makes cement.

The scenery is plain, but we need time to collect our thoughts after the excitement. The hedgerow (in August) has hawthorn, hazel, purging blackthorn, spindle, bramble, traveller's joy (soon to be old man's beard), and honeysuckle. Out of the blue there is a sign to the Robin Hood and Little John pub. Nearby at Buckmore Park is a scout camp.

Farther on, in front of a row of houses, the Way turns off the metalled road into the Blue Bell Hill picnic site, whence

Vessels on the River Medway

wc are offered a wide sweep of the Medway valley. White plasters of chalk dot the landscape. At the car park, the view is even better. Below is Burham village, while the mighty outcrop of chalk is Blue Bell Hill, handsome yet, despite many man-made scars. Kestrels, jackdaws and little owls nest in the Kentish Trust for Nature Conservation's reserve.

From the crossroads descend in front of the — need we say it? — Blue Bell pub, on a path just below the highway, down steps into a tree-lined lane, making sure not to miss Kit's Coty House. This neolithic burial chamber was built some 4,000 years ago. Nothing more than three upright stones and a great capstone remain. Yet in the eighteenth century the chamber was covered by a barrow 60 metres long. Small wonder that what survives needs to be protected from the public by iron rails.

To our right, just two minutes away, is another ancient monument, the prehistoric burial chamber known as 'The Countless Stones' — countless, because of the difficulty of knowing where the stones of the collapsed dolmen begin and end and thus of counting them. Back on the path, there are views of Maidstone, six kilometres or so southwards. We pass under the A229 dual carriageway, now hardly recognisable as a Roman road. (Buses to Maidstone from below the petrol station.) Another relic in an area rich in prehistory is the White Horse Stone, an imagination-rousing dolmen, over two metres high, marking the site of a one-time megalithic tomb. The two holes in the upper corner might, with a slice of rambler's licence, suggest a horse's head.

We mount the chalk-mottled path, turning away from the pilgrims' route into yew trees. The several paths might confuse, but stick close to the fairly narrow band of trees and keep rising. If you are not panting, you have taken the wrong path. Past more yews and out at the top, to walk around a dreary field on a plain memorable only for its pylons. The modern dolmens. Sparrows are harvesting (late August) the

Medway
Bridge

87

Nashenden Farm, near Borstal

wheat. Then inside a wood until we turn left into a field intriguingly named Frog's Rough.

Beyond Harp Farm, the way enters Boxley Wood along a muddy path, churned up by hooves. Though on the lip of the down, there are no views through the trees. We do not see the pleasant hamlet of Boxley; nor Park House, where the poet Tennyson once lived. Then out into the rain or sun, with willow-herb about, and after several stiles, a fine view of Detling, to which point the Way falls sharply. There is no underpass under the dual carriageway this time, so we make a long hairpin, ending at the Cockhorse Tavern. The church has a dexterously carved lectern, 'the finest medieval fitting in any parish church in the county,' according to Pevsner.

The North Downs Way is destined one day to climb back from here into the downs, thereupon to continue its elevated course to the sea. For the moment, however, while negotiations proceed with farmers over rights of way, it is four kilometres of the low road for us. Down from the pub and past the police station, we squeeze between two houses, at last passing through — as opposed to alongside — our first apple orchard. Now there is an ankle twister across a ploughed field, disturbing a sea of peewits, arriving not a moment too soon at St. Mary's church in Thurnham, with precise lawns and a yew which must have watched the materials being carried to the top of the downs where now only ruins mark the Norman castle. One day the North Downs Way will go past it. Thurnham takes its name from the powerful family that once ruled the roost hereabouts. The Way turns up, then right a minute later, thus missing the village (Black Horse pub and an Anglo-Saxon burial ground).

We pass an oast-house which once contained a kiln for drying hops. Beyond a riding school we turn off through the garden of a small house. One of the dogs does not like

The Countless Stones

St Mary's church, Thurnham

visitors, but the house owner has the health of walkers at heart. Though the path to Broad Street may not be exactly clear — it is, hopefully, a temporary affair — there is little room for taking the wrong turning. But wanderers may not be welcome. On a barn at Charity Farm at the entrance to Broad Street is a sign offering '£100 reward to anyone 'phoning information to the police which results in a conviction for trespass or theft from premises, woods, land or crops'. We hurry up the road from Broad Street and regain the real North Downs Way with a sigh of relief.

The vegetation is scrubby, but there are gentle views of the Weald. The rabbits don't run till you're almost on top of them. For summer outings a butterfly identification book is mandatory. A brick path passes under a delightfully cool, protective glade. We think of *A Midsummer Night's Dream,* until our reveries are disturbed by the ubiquitous pylon. Back on to true downland grass, where posts dot the hill like cairns on the Yorkshire moors. Smell of stubble burning, the scourge of insect life. Magnificent views of Hollingbourne and the Weald. We descend the well-marked path, arriving at the Pilgrims' Rest.

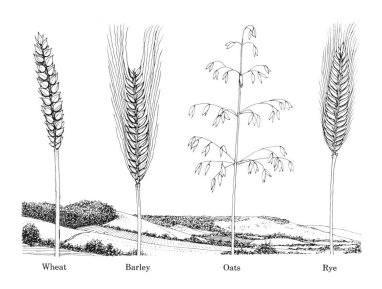

Wheat   Barley   Oats   Rye

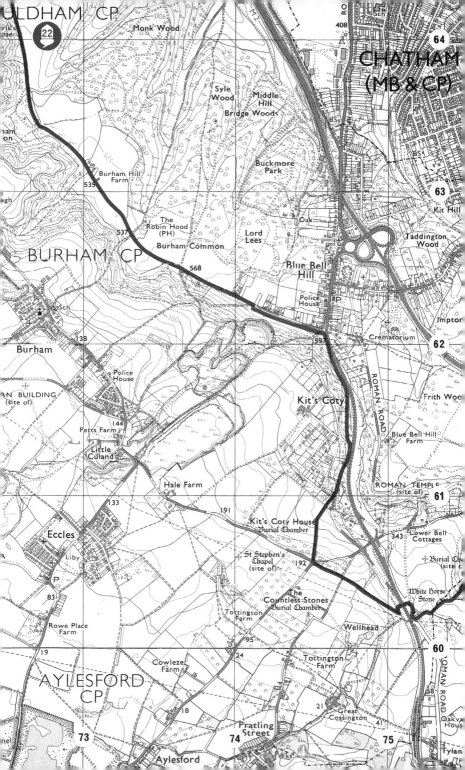

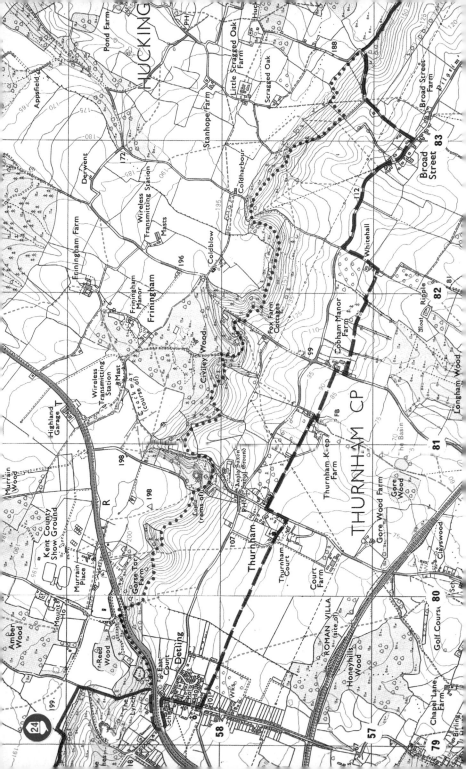

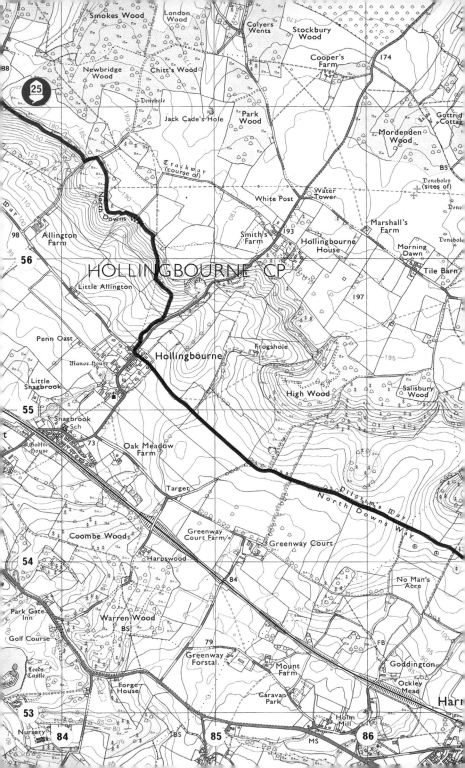

Hollingbourne to Wye

24½ kilometres

For some distance now the North Downs Way will keep to the middle ground, tantalisingly separated from the downland crest by a rippling tide of corn as we double up with the Pilgrims' Way. We have brushed up against the pilgrims' route on several occasions so far, though the exact passage of that ancient way from Winchester to Canterbury is not everywhere established beyond doubt. It is likely, however, that this section was well used in medieval times, and even before the Roman period by merchants, some of whom journeyed to the tin mines of Cornwall.

So now, with the suggestion that Geoffrey Chaucer himself passed this way, we are on a path as old as the English language. We go left at the Pilgrims' Rest pub .... Is this where the Jolly Miller bent an elbow before telling his story to that illustrious, not to say ecclesiastical, assemblage? On weekdays it is a peaceful scene, though the cast-offs of the twentieth century are strewn about ... beer cans (the Miller's?), chocolate wrappings, cigarette butts. And are the hoof-marks fossil remains of the ride to Canterbury?

Very soon the Way regains its repose. After three kilometres of extraordinarily comfortable progress, the tar reappears, and from beyond Dutch House we see the village of Harrietsham (from the Saxon, *Heregeard's hamm* or meadow), a kilometre off through the trees. A detour is worth the effort. The church (St. John the Baptist) lies between the Way and village, and has, says Pevsner, one of the finest Norman fonts in the county. Across the railway line and into the village proper, to view East Street, and in particular, Old Bell Farm, one of the best preserved Wealden cottages, dating to Tudor times.

Back to the Way, Stede Hill's Georgian house has an impressive clock tower. Thriving oaks and chestnuts in the grounds, with a great weeping beech, much like a waterfall in full torrent. Opposite Marley Court is the factory where the famed Wealden tiles were made.

Another pleasant village looms. Lenham is also less than a kilometre from the Way, and likewise has a pub and a rail connection to Ashford or London. The parish of Lenham is the source of two rivers, flowing in different directions. The

Len has been on the edge of our sights since shortly after crossing the Medway, of which it is a tributary. On its way there, the Len waters are dammed to form the lake surrounding the picturesque Leeds Castle. (See Gazetteer.) The other river, the Stour, drops towards the valley we are soon to traverse.

The detour to Lenham is at the sign 'All dogs coursing hares will BE SHOT without warning. You have been warned', where we return to the easier gravel lane. Dead ahead, though some way off, is Charing Hill. We go through a rare gate at the House of the Cross. (Coming the other way the road goes down to Lenham here.) A large cross in the field commemorates the dead of two world wars. It is maintained by the local people. A pleasant place to rest, for we are midway between the sheep-grazed down and the Wealden-edged valley.

Out of the meadow into a leafy lane and the North Downs Way returns to the tar, passing a gash in the hill near Great Pivington Farm, though vegetation makes the disused quarry less unsightly. The road north beyond the quarry leads off the Way to Warren Street. Once more on the path, there is a row of cottages facing a field of rape, an ingredient of margarine, soap and india-rubber. Lenham Chest Hospital used to treat lung complaints, indicating a dry part of the world. But the sewage works on our right might suggest otherwise.

Nettles and thistles are waiting once more past Hart Hill Farm. (These overgrown stretches could well be cleared before this book appears.) All along we can see the scabs, bruises, open wounds, cicatrices of hill quarrying. But soon the path returns to a well-worn, welcoming state. Sloes, cob-nuts, helmeted peewits, sounds of life, of people strolling up from their parked cars to Charing Hill. At Twyford House there is the chance to make a diversion, down past the A252, into the village of Charing, a visit which should be included in the itinerary.

Apart from the church of St. Peter and St. Paul (did it really house the block on which John the Baptist was beheaded?) there is a wealth of timber-framed and Georgian buildings. The Archiepiscopal Palace, now part of a farm, is another 'Henry VIII slept here' on the way to the Field of the Cloth of Gold.

Back at the waymark, the North Downs Way immediately crosses Charing Hill before following the Pilgrims' Way down a narrow metalled road between cottages, along the foot of the downs, with Wealden views once more. One and a half kilometres on, the Way skirts to the left of Burnthouse Farm, leaving the white concrete road before Beacon Hill quarry.

A snake, murky brown, admittedly only 30 centimetres long and no fatter than a large worm, dozed peaceably on the path, and made off sluggishly when tickled with a long stick.

Swallow

Yellow flag iris

Kingfisher

Reed warbler

White water-lily

Canada geese

Coot

Moorhen

Pied wagtail

97

Here is a gentle stroll through Westwell Woods, contouring the down at about 145 metres. This is ideal country for joggers, a pastime neither as dangerous nor as messy as horse-riding.

The sycamore turns to beech and there is a feeling of what this place must have looked like centuries ago. Until on the right, signs of man, with sharp falls away from the path into what looks like a disused chalk digging. Lots of paths, though not all public, go up to the top of the downs.

Soon it is tar again, and across the fields is Westwell, where the thirteenth-century church's unprepossessing exterior is no advertisement for the simple pleasures within. A first view of the railway town of Ashford. The turn-off to Westwell is at Dunn Street, a farm not quite become a hamlet. Left at the crossing and right over three stiles – watching out for splinters on the third. Now we are on a farm road separated from the shaggy down by a field where in late summer stubble sometimes smokes. Disappointed plovers pee-wit. The way to Home Farm is barred by a fierce 'No entry to public' notice, but we turn right and then left and on to grass for the first time in a long while. Next, it is a five-minute traipse across a ploughed field, sometimes helped by the tractor's tyre marks.

Climbing the stile at the other end, the notice may seem misleading, and the atmosphere forbidding. Eastwell Park is criss-crossed with public paths, all marked. But now is a chance to enjoy one of the really delicious moments of the whole walk – the ruined church of St. Mary, and Eastwell Lake. If you have poetry within you, now is the time to let it out. Plonk down under the yew tree and listen to the flapping, quacking, guffawing, jeering, mocking, friendly noises from this enchanting open-air aviary. The fish and insects, the reeds, lilies, bulrushes attract Canada geese, moorhens, mallards, coots, kingfishers, reed warblers, hedge warblers, swans, wagtails, while swallows and swifts hawk for food overhead. Imagine ducks from all over Kent and the South East deciding on their summer holiday – yeah, let's go to Eastwell, the lake district of British birdlife.

Lombardy poplars line the way. Sheep, green-branded 'EP' for Eastwell Park, graze in a field reached through a kissing gate. Watch out for another kissing gate on to the road, and yet another into a field with more 'EP' lambs. Head for the red-brick wall, where even another of these permissive exits takes us into Boughton Lees (many places in Kent are 'lees', which here probably means a tranquil place). The green is truly English, with the cricket pitch and the pavilion, overlooked by the Flying Horse Inn and houses which double as grandstands in the summer. The cricket club has taken out insurance against windows broken at square leg ... and some home owners have been paid out.

In the distance is the church of Boughton Aluph, but quite soon we reach the fork where we have to choose the route to

Lombardy poplars at Eastwell Park

the sea. Is it the way of the spirit, to Canterbury, or the way of the flesh, to Folkestone and Dover? The third waymark points back to Farnham. We go right, leaving the Pilgrims' Way, soon turning into a field bordering a large orchard where a farmer and his wife harvested the Worcester Pearmain (in mid-September) from low-slung trees. The Cox had to wait a bit longer. (See page 119 for Canterbury loop.)

The Way zigzags across the fields, over the road and a stile into Perry Court Farm, where attention should be paid to the acorn signs, which keep us out of the strawberry patches. From the farm, the path drops gently between cultivated fields, goes through a cabbage patch and enters Wye over a cattle grid.

Across the railway line and over the bridge at the Tickled Trout pub, we cross the Great Stour, on its way from Ashford to Canterbury and the Channel. It is the first river we have met that does not run into the Thames or its estuary. Here the Stour is a ten-metre-wide stripling, firmly controlled by a lock. Beyond is the racecourse. Coffee shops and pubs abound and there are train connections to the outside world.

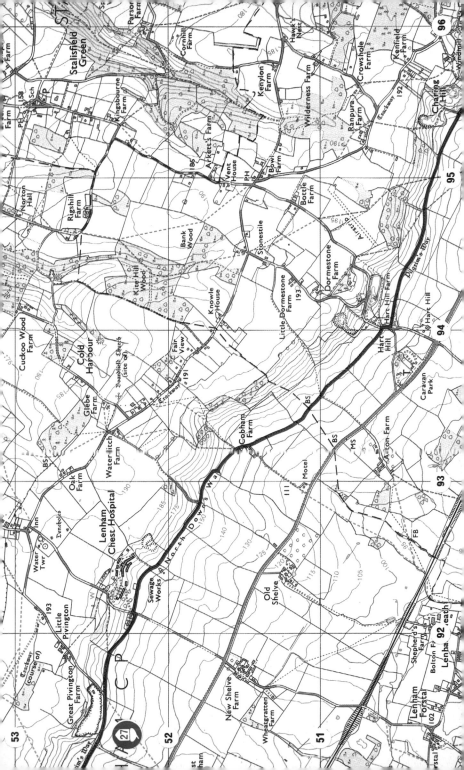

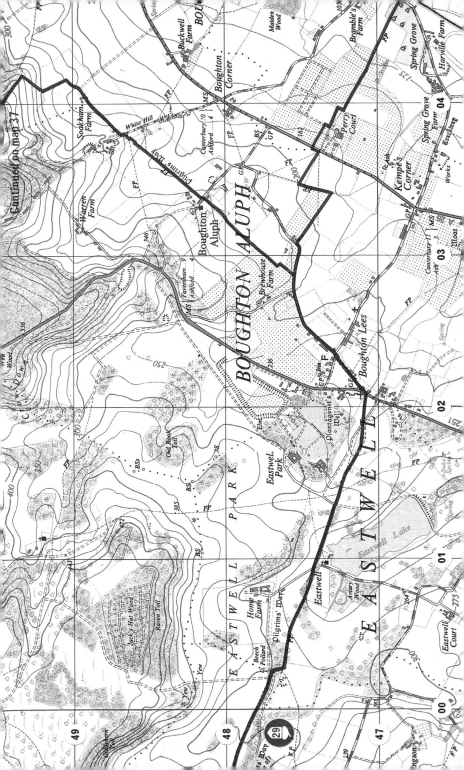

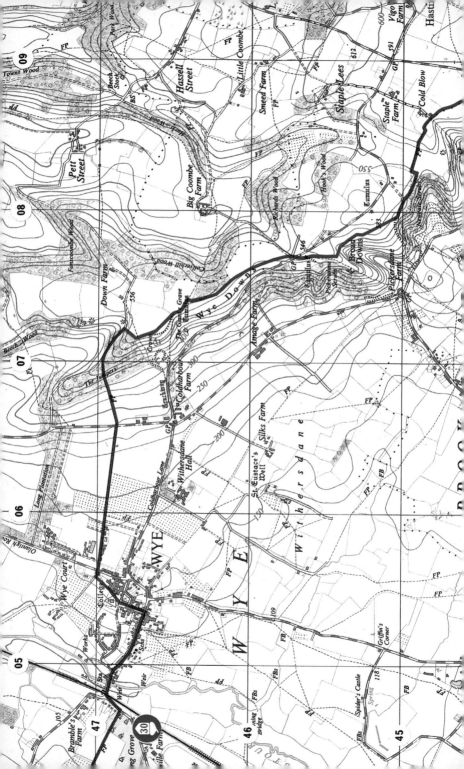

Wye to Folkestone and Dover

35½ kilometres

The Way leaves the centre of Wye through the churchyard, past the College of St. Gregory and St. Martin, founded in the 1400s by a local lad, John Kempe, later Archbishop of Canterbury. Up Occupation Road, through the grounds of the agricultural college, a faculty of the University of London. Here are the laboratories where hops, like Wye Target, which has a greater resistance to disease, are developed. There are some ancient buildings as well, and patches of runner beans, onions, sweetcorn, calabrese, courgettes, and beetroot being subjected to rigorous experimentation. The college has an interpretive exhibition open to the public. And so, on to the Wye Downs.

From The Junipers, turn right along a minor road, peering into a deep, silent valley which could have been transported intact from the Yorkshire Dales. But we turn right over stiles and back into the meadow. The path picks a way through sheep and cattle, and concrete slits, now overgrown, no doubt where the Home Guard lay in wait for the *Luftwaffe*.

The picture postcard at our feet has a dreamlike quality the river valley, town and hamlets, the colourful quilt of the fields, stretched between the hedgerows and trees without which the natural life of the countryside is difficult to sustain.

At the road, where two gates are difficult to lift, we cross the road and enter the Wye and Crundale Downs Nature Reserve, established by the Nature Conservancy Council. The 100 hectares of chalk downland and woodland are here preserved in their virgin state. Almost a museum, but not quite, as modern agriculture wreaks havoc on the downs of southern England. The feature of this reserve, which runs for 2½ kilometres along the scarp of the downs, is the Devil's Kneading Trough, a dry valley or coomb cut steeply 60 metres into the chalk. It was here that the North Downs Way was officially opened in the summer of 1978.

The official booklet on the reserve explains the trough's origins and how the downs protrude as they do: 'You are standing on a thin layer of soil overlying a massive thickness of chalk. Although the chalk is soft, it is harder than the clay and other rocks of the region and therefore resists weather-

Devil's Kneading Trough

ing better'. Some 10,000 years ago, 'the ground would have been deeply frozen and therefore shattered by frost in winter. During spring thaws, much of the shattered material probably slid down the sides of the coomb and was carried away by the water from melting snowfields on the crest of the downs'. The 'kneading' comes from the horizontal paths worn by sheep and cattle.

There is a nature trail quite close to the Way, where are found the usual and the rare – 27 species of butterfly, 17 of orchid, including the lady orchid (or Maid of Kent), the black-veined moth, the willow warbler (feeding at the tips of branches in the scrub in early summer) and that hyena of the woods, the green woodpecker. Adders are fairly common too.

From Broad Downs, above the trough, we see below us the surprisingly well-preserved one-street manorial village of Brook, its ribbon of houses and gardens dominated by the early Norman church. At the double stile past Cold Blow Farm, resist the temptation to go over the second, bearing half left instead, across the middle of the field to the road. Ten minutes on, the road swings down to Hastingleigh (pronounced 'lie'), but we turn left for a short distance to a gate which leads to a comfortable trackway.

This is a narrow downs top, with views on both sides. At an open gate the path seems as though it should continue through, but a rambler's arrow directs us to the right, inside the field, down to another road. Is there a smell of the sea, or does the imagination play tricks? The triangulation point, standing (sometimes, in late summer) in a field of rape, measures 584 feet (175 metres), whence views of Brabourne and Lord Brabourne's country house, Mersham-Le-Hatch, beyond. Descend sharply. If thirsty, the Brabourne village pub is an easy drop down – but a stiff trek back, remember.

Otherwise, the North Downs Way continues soberly

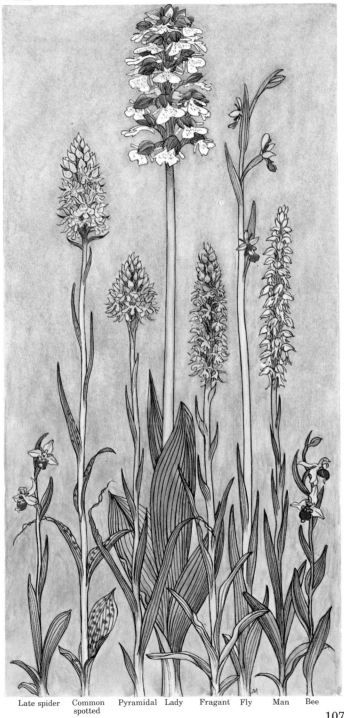

Late spider   Common   Pyramidal   Lady   Fragant   Fly   Man   Bee
                       spotted

through an acorn gate on the left at the hairpin bend, and keeping the fence to the right, moves into a path where pheasant may be seen. Secateurs, to cut the occasional brambles. Descend, under a sparking pylon, to the metalled road, and we turn down to the village of Stowting, past the telephone box at Fidding Lane. Here, the Way runs just inside the field. Note the tiled barns at Stowting Court. And the delectable mermaid on the sign of the Anchor Inn. The appropriately named Water Farm produces a brook which runs into the Stour.

Turn left off the road and up a chalky path on Cobb's Hill and sit on a stile, casting around at the world. Bales of hay in a field below, next door a shepherd and two lively Welsh border collies fuss over grazing sheep – thatched barns, pylons, cattle, a farmyard, and smudged in the distance, now some way off, Brabourne. And at eye level, hill-top farms, furrowed fields, dead thistle heads like Ben Gunn's hair-do.

At the double stile, go up along the fence, left. Here are more lambs, now (mid-September) reaching yearling-hood, and soon to be called tegs, or in the meat trade, hoggets. Rams, from 12 weeks to 18 months are called wethers, if castrated. There is a mix of breeds here – the black-headed are Suffolks, while the white-faced are Kent or Romney Marsh, found mostly in the south-eastern counties. We are, incidentally, at the nearest point to Romney Marsh.

The Way keeps close to the road, sometimes on a path, but often picking through a field. The road is Stone Street, built by the Romans to link Canterbury (*Durovernum*) with Lympne (*Portus Lemanis*), no longer a port for the simple reason that the sea has receded. (Farthing Common on the left has a parking area.)

We are on a hog's back, but before the down starts its descent, climb over a high stile, crossing the road into a field of corn. Ahead is the *sea* – azure, menacing, choppy, perhaps even hidden in the fog, but the English Channel all the same.

Descend under a pylon, keeping dead ahead at the chalk gash (and not right up the hillock). We curve round the down, and as there are several paths, it is advisable to keep near to the top. Climbing one stile, we have a vignette of Page's Farm below, with its curiously placed church in the farmyard. A fine pastoral scene. Now head for Staple Farm, the wireless station to the right. Acorns and yellow arrows point the direction.

At the road, Postling is announced, with a cheval rampant, and *Invicta* (undefeated), the county war cry, reminding us that not even William defeated the people of Kent. (Though he gave much of it to his half-brother, Bishop Odo of Bayeux, all the same.)

Up the lane, past the 'Out of bounds to troops' sign, climbing to Etchinghill, carefully skirting the rubbish dump. Here it started to rain and I opened my umbrella, a much-maligned tool of the walker's trade. In summer or early

Page's Farm, Postling

autumn, it is easier than putting on a sweaty oilskin. Just
below the wireless station, climb the low fence. Round the
back, the North Downs Way crosses the Saxon Shore Way, a
new Kent Rights of Way Council walk along the ancient
coastline. The Saxon Shore Way goes on to the Military
Canal at West Hythe, but we turn left into a Ministry of
Defence training area, with a reminder that explosives,
blank cartridges and the like might be used. The warning
adds 'This path is likely to be used by troops under training'.
I found gorse the most hazardous obstacle. The path mean-
ders through a wood, over roots – with cuckoo–pint about – to
the road under the pylon. Etchinghill village has a hospital, a
pub, and a succession of bungalows lining the B2065 main
road, which should be crossed, before going up the lane and
over the stile into a field down to a yellow-painted stile and so
under the bridge of the disused railway. We come out where
the pylons meet. The Way is up the floor of this lovely valley,
reaching a stile at the fence. If coming the other way, there is
a Defence warning not to touch anything — 'It may explode
and kill you'. But all is quiet.

The muddy path descends through Hungar Lane, then
rounds a coomb, whence views back of the wireless station,
Summerhouse Hill, Asholt Wood and the hamlet of Pean at
our feet. To the right are Folkestone housing estates and the
sweep of the coast beyond. The waymark is buried in grass,
but it indicates that for the moment the route is below the
chalk pit. The locals walk above the quarry, avoiding the
narrow tar road, where cars race by. It has a fine array of
wild flowers, and a stone proclaiming 'Borough of Folkestone
Castle, Mayor 1934'. One and a half kilometres on, turning
on to the grass of Cheriton Hill, we bird's-eye the harbour
town of Folkestone.

Several paths come and go, but we follow the one alongside the road, while watching out for protruding roots. The Folkestonians prefer to come here by car. Cherry Garden Hill has an apron of green sticking out over the town, ideal for model airplanes and kite flying. A narrow lane leads alongside the waterworks property. Yelping and howling to the left are from quarantine kennels, where the impatient tenants are registering their contempt for Britain's (essential) anti-rabies regulations. A new footpath runs parallel to the road behind the hedge.

Over a stile and towards Castle Hill, or is it a camouflaged fort with remnants of Caesar's army waiting to be stormed? Under the pylon and climb along the side, and there is an all-embracing view of the harbour, ferry boats, and, on Copt Point, a martello tower, one of 25 built along the coast from Folkestone to Littlestone as a defence against possible French invasion. This one went up in 1806, as Napoleon prepared to cross from Boulogne with his *Grande Armée.* The circular towers, styled on forts at Cape Martella in Corsica, are two storeys high, with walls up to two metres thick, and spaced at half-kilometre intervals, enough to keep the enemy within gun range. But they didn't arrive.

Skirting Castle Hill, we come at last to the first 'Bed and Breakfast' actually on the Way. We go round Round Hill. If the profusion of paths confuses, simply maintain height. It is no bad thing in popular places if various paths are used, as this reduces erosion. Cross the lively A260 to Canterbury, climb the lane opposite and look out for a stile on your right. From this path on Creteway Down there is a fine view of Sugarloaf Hill, though without the feel of its Brazilian namesake. At the Valiant Sailor pub, the finger-post announces that there remain 5½ miles (8½ kilometres) to Dover.

The lane next to the pub once again crosses the Saxon Shore Way. We have officially reached the sea, though it is far below. The fall is truly vertiginous, and the walker would do well, after a regulation squiz over the edge, to face left and proceed well inland. The white cliffs, the sea and France, 35 kilometres across *La Manche,* in good weather, or bad. A path drops off the Way to The Warren, a gault clay outcrop layered with fossils at the base of the cliffs. It is also rich in birdlife, including migrant warblers and flycatchers, and in winter, members of the auk family. The kittiwake gull breeds on the cliffs near Dover. The herring gull is everywhere, breeding inland in winter at rubbish dumps.

To our dismay, the cliff-top path drops 50 or so steps, to go up instantly on the other side of the chasm. After which it is right at the acorn behind a house ('Eagle's Nest') along the fenced path. The pillboxes were anti-aircraft defences in the Battle of Britain. Man's humanity to man is restored by the cottage owners of Capel-le-Ferne village who mow the green verges of the North Downs Way. The wind blows *from* the sea and our hats are secure.

After 1½ kilometres on the cliffs, we reach the yellow-painted tea kiosk at Capel Court, which is open in dry weather. Also open at various times are the country club, the Royal Oak and a café.The ample path leads on the sea side of the caravan park. Behind Abbotscliff House we see if the red flag is up, indicating that the Lydden Spout Rifle Range is active. In which case the walker must take the alternative path which runs parallel with the A20 as far as the Plough, and then climbs to rejoin the coastal route outside the firing range.

If in luck — and firing happens only occasionally — we can stick to the stony road, which becomes a track over Abbot's Cliff. The Folkestone-Dover railway disappears into a tunnel far beneath us. More huge fossils of destruction — concrete slabs, steel girders, man-made castles, and also, hewn on the chalky cliff-side by the weather, buttresses like Buddhist gompas perched on a Himalayan mountain path.

The rifle range targets are like giant Aunt Sallies, numbered one to 24. Then we are rejoined by the 'red flag' diversion. The Way runs between the Great Farthingloe strip (National Trust) and the reappeared railway line and the Groynes 120 metres below on the sea side. A glimpse of Dover harbour's Admiralty and Prince of Wales piers. We descend. Is this the last of our ups and downs? No. One more climb, along Shakespeare Cliff, so named because just about here, the sightless Gloucester jumped 'from the dread summit of this chalky bourne' and survived to ask 'but have I fall'n, or no?' (*King Lear,* Act IV Scene IV). Somewhere below, almost as mythical, diggings mark the spot where the Channel Tunnel may one day enter the sea. A Dover stone announces: 'Pepper, Mayor, 1095/6'. The whole town rises up. At night the lights are blinding and without a torch the walker may lose his way. The harbour, castle, more white cliffs.

Before our goal is reached, sink on to a bench whence to regard the hard-worked-for destination at leisure. Then down a made-up path past allotments to the finish (or the start) at Sunny Corner, Aycliff. The house, owned for four generations by the Pidgeon family, has a garden of remembrance on the spot where, in the 1939-45 war, was a dug-out with machine guns covering the beach. No pub in sight, but a short and regular bus run into *Dubris*.

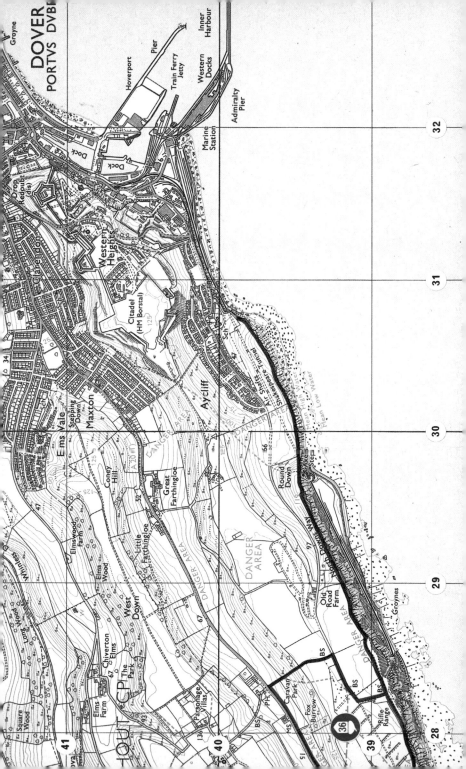

Godmersham Park

Chilham Castle

The Way via Canterbury-Boughton Lees to Canterbury

21 kilometres

The North Downs Way loop to Canterbury and the sea at Dover leaves off between the Boughtons. Best to start at Boughton Lees, walk the half-kilometre and fork left, past orchards, to Boughton Aluph, where the flint church seems far away from a potential congregation. In the thirteenth century it was a lively place, its fireplace certainly used as a hearth for passing pilgrims. Not surprisingly, much of our route is now shared with the Pilgrims' Way. It rises gently, crossing a metalled road at an overgrown cottage on White Hill. From the farm road, there are handsome views of Wye and the downs beyond. We wind past Soakham Farm, before climbing breathfully under yews along a whitened path into a forest of beech. Soakham Downs is a rather wild place, and wet too, as its name suggests, in the short rainy season.

A small grassed mound is at the high point, wired off from the world. Is it an ancient burial site? We are in Challock Forest, most of which belongs to the Forestry Commission. There is bracken and birch under an arboreal alleyway through King's Wood. Our boots crunch on the chestnut leaves, silencing the birds. A bit deeper into the coniferous part of the forest the distinctive 'churring' of the nightjar may be heard in the May twilight. The Way is well marked as we keep all the while to the highest point of the down, through a vast coppice of chestnut saplings. Deeper in the trees breed the fallow deer which were introduced to England by the Saxons and range far west into Ashdown Forest. Below is Godmersham Park, where Jane Austen's brother Edward lived in the Palladian mansion.

Beyond the Forestry Commission board the path forks. Thanks to vandals, the directional signs had disappeared when I passed by, but carry straight on, ignoring the path to the left. Often, as here, when an unmarked fork seems to offer equally glowing possibilities, a thoughtful rambler has placed a tree trunk or large branch across the wrong one. Five minutes on, we drop into a beech-lined lane, once more dry and chalky under foot. In autumn, spiders spin webs

Chilham village

across the path from branch to branch. Past oast-houses at Hurst Farm. We trample hazel cobs, skirting a vast beech-fringed field, down to the metalled road.

All the while, the Great Stour has been a kilometre or so to our right in its bed below. We shall next meet it in Canterbury. Above the river are the downs named after Julliberrie's Grave, a long barrow with a burial chamber dating to the New Stone Age settlers 50 centuries before.

The row of cottages is called, collectively, Mountain Street, though one house with Tudor beams is Moncton Manor. A high brick wall — and guard dogs — enclose Chilham Castle. Watch out, in mid-October, for the bees feasting on the ivy. The road leads up to the square at Chilham, one of the architectural jewels of our hike. And it concludes as refreshing an eight-kilometre stroll as one may find anywhere in all Britain's isles.

We sit in the sun outside the White Horse eyeing tourists on this mandatory call on their tour of Canterbury and surrounds. There are antique shops and chichi restaurants, and too many cars. But the two-storey beamed buildings are well preserved. A road drops steeply from each corner of the miniscule square. Chilham was founded in AD182 by Lucius, the first Christian king in England. The castle has been owned by nine English kings over the years, and of course Henry VIII dined here in the lively company of lute players and 'fayre' companions, after deer hunting and falconry in the grounds.

The castle gate is open every day except Monday and Friday (unless they are bank holidays) for visits to the Capability Brown gardens, the Battle of Britain Museum and the Birds of Prey Centre. There are public jousting tournaments in the summer.

A notice in St. Mary's church porch explains that 'as much

of the village used to be owned by the castle, the church was doubtless filled every Sunday with tenants and servants behind the gentry of the time. The present owner, the Viscount Massereene and Ferrard, is patron of the living, but regularity of attendance now depends on the conscience of the individual.' Other times, other customs.

In the churchyard a hollowed-out yew, for ten centuries a-growing, produces healthy berries yet.

The Way leads out of the churchyard gate down to and across the A252, then up past more orchards, where (in mid-October) Spartan apples are being harvested, and so in front of the thatched buildings of Cork Farm to Old Wives Lees. For the first time since setting off from Farnham we have left the Areas of Outstanding Natural Beauty, which aim to protect the landscape from unnecessary development. We leave the village, with its converted oast-houses, follow the signpost to Canterbury and Chartham, and in less than one kilometre go left at the end of the row of cottages — at Pamphletti's Cottage, to be exact.

The North Downs Way descends through orchards of Golden Delicious and Cox. An avenue of limes shelters the fruit from the wind and the walker from the fruit. Chartham village is half-right across the river. Another stile leads into a hopfield, now bare, the poles and connecting wires waiting for next year's planting. A row of beeches, a bumpy white field, more orchards and left at the next stile (sometimes the finger-post is turned straight down — do not swallow the mischief).

The farm road leads to the railway line, which should be crossed with care, especially after a train has passed. This is the London to Dover line, with Faversham and Selling the nearest stations. The Way passes through the A. W. Arnold family farm. In mid-October, workers are picking Crispins, the second-last apples to go. Ida's Reds, the last, certainly in this area, are ready and waiting. Now a concrete road winds through the farm, the better to harvest cleanly and quickly. Fright Wood is on the left. On arriving at Hatch Farm, go right past the bakery (a converted oast-house) and through the gate on to the road. Thence, immediately right up New Town Street, past the Chapter Arms, its dovecotes and red-hot pokers, to Chartham Hatch.

In the village, bear left at the road junction and quickly move right, down the metalled lane, Nightingale Close, which runs past the football field into chestnuts, holly, more apple trees, on a descending path. It is a pleasant walk through Howfield Wood, which turns off near the end of an orchard on to a clear path through more chestnuts. On our right are the gentle tree-covered lines of Bigbury Camp, the Belgic settlement which pre-dated the founding of Canterbury by the Romans.

Carry straight on, across the new A2, plunging away from the motorised noises into more orchards and hopfields, where

Dovecote at the Chapter Arms, Chartham Hatch

a wooden foot-bridge crosses a stream. The Way passes the National Trust property, Golden Hill, and soon makes contact with the first houses of Canterbury proper, in the suburb of Harbledown. At the bottom of the lane is the dual carriageway to Faversham. Countryside Commission paths are not defined through towns, so from the roundabout waymark the purist walker will wish to go the whole hog into the city centre. Now the cathedral becomes visible. From this approach, it is unlike some other great English cathedrals, Salisbury in particular, whose spire proclaims its presence leagues away.

To avoid the traffic on Rheims Way, cross the roundabout by the subway, then go off right down to the railway line (this is the West Canterbury, Chartham, Chilham, Wye line). Over the foot-bridge the path at last meets the Stour, previously encountered at Wye. It does not seem to have grown very much. The old city is entered at Westgate, now straddling the London Road. Once, in days of greater insecurity, a drawbridge guarded the river. From there, it's down the High Street to the cafés and the cathedral.

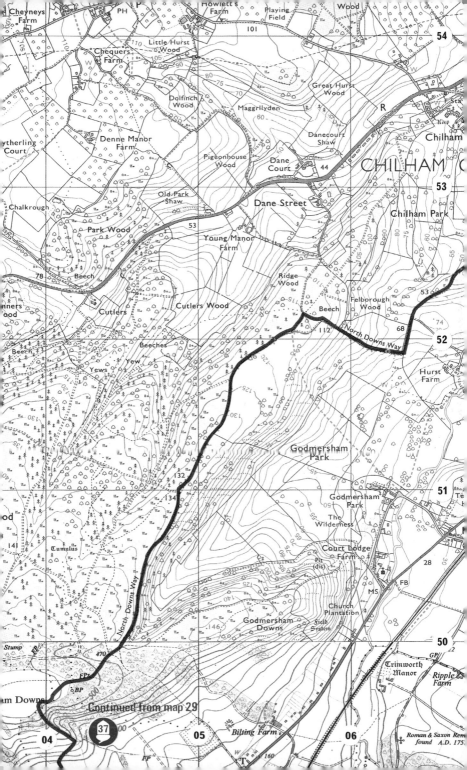

Continued from map 29

37

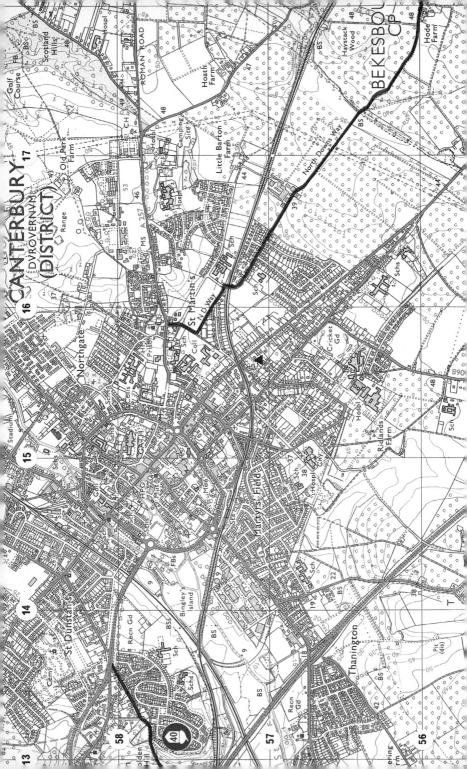

Canterbury to Dover

30 kilometres

We leave Canterbury on foot, for there is no real saving in taking the bus to our starting point. Traffic harassment is minimal, and on the way eastward, we have the opportunity to see the remains of St. Augustine's Abbey (early fourteenth century) and the 'County Gaol and House of Correction', before turning off Longport at the waymark into Spring Lane. Past sports-fields, over the railway, alongside new houses, and Chaucer Close, on to a metalled bridleway. We enter Little Barton Farm, through its seemingly never-ending orchards of pears, plums and apples. On the left, just before the second pylon, is a nursery for trees destined to embellish motorways — sycamores and rowans. We finally leave the orchards, still on the tar, alongside an anti-scrumper fence of alders.

Hode Lane runs under beech, ash and sycamore into Patrixbourne, the entrance to which is marked by a house with a fine ornamental yew hedge. The village has a feel of the French Midi about it — wavy roofs, a barn on the roadside, but only one reddening cherry tree, and that one ornamental. Patrixbourne is cut off from the world by high trees. Its great treasure is the Norman church, one of the finest in Kent. Look out for the skilfully carved tympanum (that's the space between the door lintel and the arch above).

We go out of the village, and at the last house scratch the moss from the waymark to discover that it points round the fields. We are off the hard surface for the first time since Canterbury. Rabbits to the left, heavy lorries to the right on the new bypass which cuts us off from the village of Bridge. A Saxon burial ground is in the wood, but we keep on towards the road. Now there is nearly a kilometre of unpleasant perambulation alongside the highway. We look skywards, purse our lips. This is the A2, the Roman road known as Watling Street. Highland Court, on the left, is a hospital. Under the bridge, but off our route, is the road to Bishops-bourne, where Joseph Conrad lived in the rectory.

Beyond the bridge (which do not cross) the path drops to road level, but soon turns off through a gate into a field, crossing it diagonally. There now follows some of the dreariest progress of the North Downs Way — a succession of ploughed and grazed fields on the lower side of Barham Downs, linked by a series of yellow- and green-painted poles. The soil is white and you are Lawrence of Arabia loping across the desert. In summer it is thick with corn. We draw gently away from the A2. Upper Digges Place Farm comes as merciful relief.

From the farm the Way continues between hedgerows to the cemetery, crosses the road to Aylesham, and soon onwards through a farmyard to Womenswold, or more exactly *Wymynswold, wymyn* being the Old English for women. Pleasant Georgian cottages close to the church. This is the nearest point to the village of Aylesham, built in the twenties for the workers at Snowdown colliery. More fields and a couple of gates lead us less than a kilometre later into Woolage Village. Outside the grocery shop is a North Downs Way finger-post which despite its height of two metres was covered by snow for three weeks in the heavy winter of 1979. No orchards up here.

For some time now the chimneys of the Snowdown colliery have been in our vision. But farther around are two white chimneys which were part of a factory making breezeblocks from coal products. Such was the pollution that the villagers mounted a campaign and had it closed down. They claimed immediate improvement in their health and that of their children.

Follow that once-smothered sign across the field, via stiles, to a gate. Briefly on to the tar on a path through a hazel coppice along Three Barrows Down. The Way is raised above the fields, as if specially constructed that way. Tumuli to the right. From the railway bridge, looking south, we can see Shepherdswell station as the line enters a tunnel. Divert north-east for Barfreston church (see Gazetteer). Follow the tar for nearly one kilometre towards Eythorne, but turn off before at Longlane Farm, whence, after negotiating a series of kissing gates, we briefly regain the metalled road, before going over a level-crossing of the disused East Kent railway line. We shall cross it again later, on its way to a disused coal mine.

We are poised to enter Shepherdswell (or Sibertswold, as some will anciently have it) but turn left immediately and climb a track and then cross fields and a string of stiles behind a row of houses to Moon Hill on the upper reaches of the village. The Way continues modestly next to a lock-up garage opposite the school in Mill Lane. In the potato fields descend, under the pylon, crossing into the next field at an overgrown patch, and then slanting down to the stile. The stiles hereabouts are rickety and could be dangerous. It seems to be a section of the walk that has not yet caught the imagination of the public. We cross the disused railway — the rails have been taken up — once more and veer left behind Coldred church which is small, has indications of Saxon and Norman origins, and stands on a large earthwork.

Tympanum on the Norman church at Patrixbourne

Plunge into the trees at the post box on the crossroads. Soon we enter the grounds of Waldershare House, the Earl of Guildford's home. But before reaching the mansion, we see the splendid Palladian-style belvedere (built in 1725 at a cost of £1,703 7s 4d) half-dressed in greenery. A very wise folly indeed, if pure joy to the onlooker was the architect's intention. Across acorn signs and fields of lucerne, almost to the doorstep of the Queen Anne house. It has many windows, looking like an eighteenth-century secondary modern school.

Twin platoons of lime trees run immaculately off the east side, as we pass on the left of the house. Just beyond the garages go left, then right along the estate drive. At the crossroads we enter a meadow in the middle of which is an extraordinary arbour — yew, beech, oak — and no larger than the floor of the Royal Albert Hall. It looks a very ancient place. We come to the road at the church, through a spacious kissing gate in which Two Ton Tessie could comfortably embrace both Laurel and Hardy together. Sadly, All Saint's Church, like Coldred's, has to be locked up for reasons of security.

The Waldershare porter's gates and lodge are a minute's walk off the Way, but we go through another kissing gate and across the fields to Minacre Farm. Yellow plastic arrows point the diagonal track across cultivated land. The metalled road winds past cottages to the village of Ashley (no pub). It is caravanning country, as can be seen from the red flags and the ubiquitous 'CC' sign (for 'Caravan Club').

We have turned southwards, and from now on run virtually straight into Dover. On reaching the hedge, we glance back at a peaceful scene of twentieth-century rural England. Incidentally, if the farmer has not cut the sides of his hedge, you may step a pace into the field. Better than tearing clothes on the hawthorn.

And so to the Roman road. This one connected Dover with Richborough (*Rutupiae*), one of the original forts of the Saxon Shore. Its straightness apart, there have been important changes on this ancient artery. Now it is metalled, and the chariots are automated while, instead of togas, citizens of the empire are clothed in blue jeans.

We carry on through the crossroads at Maydensole Farm, soon forking left along a marked path. The wind is chilly alongside Cane Wood (in early November), but there are clumps of red poppies and daisies in the fields. We may be lucky enough to see the cinnamon-coloured hoopoe, or hear its 'hoo-hoo-hoo'. This striking bird occasionally loses its way across the Channel in mid-summer.

A rubbish tip, undated, greets us 1½ kilometres farther on at the next crossroads. It is, happily, often cleared. The road runs off the Way (right) to the village of Whitfield, and more closely to Church Whitfield.

At Pineham Farm the Way hiccoughs round and back to the Roman road. Wood-pigeons feed on unpicked apples. Watch out for a stiff and lop-sided gate, followed by a muddy, mucky lane, where the scattered red bricks and breezeblocks do not suggest classical origins. A broken stile and into a grassy meadow with cows and sheep. We cross the new A2. The path is overgrown once more. To the left, the clock tower of the Duke of York's Royal Military School in Guston. And then, ahead, Dover Castle and the Strait of Dover.

The North Downs Way makes its last drop, gently at first, to the tar (the Roman road sign points in the direction from which we have just come), and then more sharply. Under Long Hill are mowed fields, nice for a first or last swig or a Chaucerian stanza. We cross the railway line, past Danes Court, white berries in the hedge, old man's beard, and Charlton cemetery. There are three cemeteries here, but we keep on descending. The last — or first — waymark for the North Downs Way is at the side of the entrance to St. Mary's cemetery, next to the Charlton C of E primary school. Ramblers with energy remaining may turn up sharp left here for a visit to the castle. Others may amble into town for a cup of tea, or even catch the ferry for some walking on the other side. But the North Downs Way is officially over. In one direction at least.

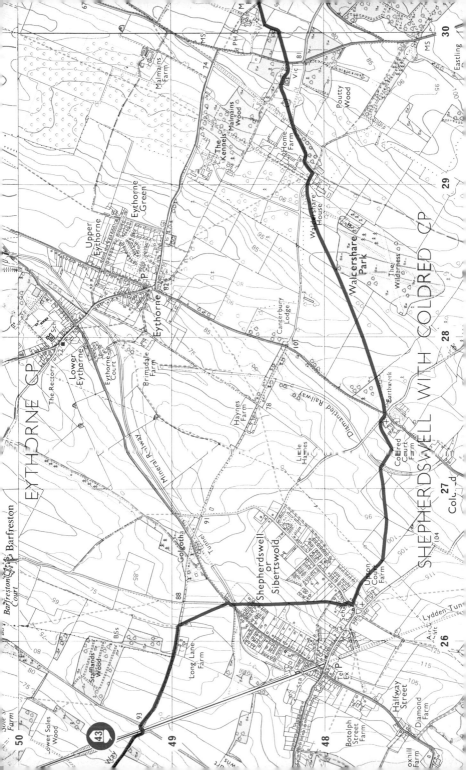

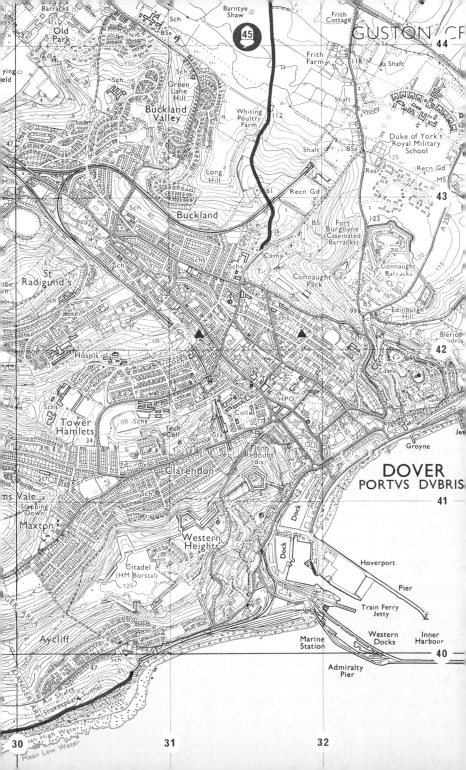

Towns on or near the Way

SURREY

Guildford – The cobbled High Street is a jumble of styles, ancient and modern, falling to the Wey and highlighted by the Guildhall, 'superb, the epitome of Restoration panache' (Ian Nairn in the Pevsner Surrey), its 1683 clock hanging cheekily over the busy traffic. Higher up, the early Jacobean Abbot's Hospital once housed 12 men and eight women. Lewis Carroll of Wonderland fame used to visit the family home, The Chestnuts, in Castle Hill. The Norman keep is all that really remains of the castle in this ancient town. Now, with a post-war cathedral, university and Yvonne Arnaud Theatre, it has become an important cultural and tourist centre.

Dorking – Market town granted its charter by Edward I. Bow-fronted shop windows, winding thoroughfares and a well-proportioned High Street.

Reigate Some remains of Norman castle at the north end of the High Street, opposite the Augustinian Priory (1235), which later became a Tudor mansion. Market town linked with Redhill, a child of the railway age.

KENT

Sevenoaks – Pleasant town with some Georgian houses and a fifteenth-century grammar school. On the southern outskirts, in a deer park, is Knole (National Trust), one of the largest private houses in England. A Tudor hall, and many other rooms with furniture, rugs, tapestries and paintings. Visits: various opening hours April to September; phone Sevenoaks 53006.

Rochester – The most imposing of the Medway towns is dominated by the great Norman castle, with the tallest tower keep in England, 38 metres of ragstone to the top of the corner-turrets. The cathedral has a large Early English crypt and fourteenth-century murals, in addition to the pair of fine doorways. The lady chapel is now the chapel of King's School. Well-preserved tombs of medieval bishops. It is *Edwin Drood*

High Street, Guildford

Knole, near Sevenoaks

country, with Charles Dickens' Swiss Chalet in the grounds of Eastgate House.

Merges with **Chatham,** the dockyard and Royal Arsenal, which two and a half centuries ago caused the passing Daniel Defoe to describe it as 'the most considerable of the kind in the world'. As a boy (1817-21), Dickens lived in Ordnance Terrace, now fronted by the railway station. Earliest flying-boat landings in the estuary.

Maidstone – From *Meghanstone* (mighty stone) or *Maydonstone* (town of maidens), you take your choice. The agricultural capital and county town astride the Medway. Still some hop gardens and breweries. Flemish religious refugees brought linen thread manufacture in the sixteenth century. Along the river, the area around All Saints, a church in the perpendicular style, has the remains of a fourteenth-century college, while the palace, mostly Elizabethan, was once the residence of the Archbishop of Canterbury. Museum and art gallery in (Elizabethan) Chillington Manor has relics of William Hazlitt, born in the town in 1778. The town hall is a fine eighteenth-century building, while nearby Bank Street has examples of ornamental plasterwork called pargeting. But surviving charms are rapidly being obscured by office tower blocks.

Canterbury – A settlement since prehistory, the Romans found *Belgae* already living there. The walls date to the third century, and large chunks survive. The West Gate has a museum of armour. Original building on cathedral site was destroyed by fire in 1067. After which, the first cathedral was built, of which parts of crypt and wall and nave ground-plan survive. Thomas à Becket was murdered in the north-west transept (1170) and the site of his shrine is in Trinity Chapel. The Black Prince is buried in the cathedral. The new cathedral is the first English example of Gothic pointed, as

The old palace, Maidstone

opposed to Norman rounded, arches. Leaving the town on the east side, the walker passes the impressive remains of St. Augustine's Abbey, and St. Martin's, the oldest working church in England, where Queen Bertha prayed in St. Augustine's day. Izaak Walton was married in St. Mildred's. Fine sixteenth-century weavers' houses overlook the Stour in St. Peter's Street. County cricket ground and University of Kent.

Folkestone – Channel port, with connections to Ostend, Calais, Boulogne. Much of the town was destroyed by Second World War bombs. The Warren, below the North Downs Way, between cliff and sea, has a fascinating habitat of rare plants, fossil remains and fine trees. There, too, is evidence of Roman villas, indicating the town's antiquity. Church of St. Mary and St. Eanswythe, Early English, has a sanctuary worth seeing. Folkestone was a 'limb' of the Cinque Ports — it supplied one ship to Dover's quota, but was still put to the torch by the French, aided by the Scots, in 1378. Defoe later described it as a 'miserable fishing town'. Then, one day in 1853, it was rescued by the arrival of the South-Eastern Railway. Handsome Victorian and Edwardian houses mark its resurgence as a resort town. Dickens holidayed at 3 Albion Villas (now Copperfield House) while writing *Little Dorrit*. He climbed the cliffs with Wilkie Collins. H. G. Wells, resident of Spade House, now a museum, wrote *Kipps* and *The History of Mr. Polly* here.

Dover – Channel port and ferry terminus crammed between white cliffs and downs. Dover beach has been celebrated in poetry by Matthew Arnold. Romans built walls to protect *Dubris*, but it was a port of entry — and resistance — well before. The Painted House, recently opened, is a rare Roman gem. Dover Castle is the dominating man-made edifice, imposingly situated on the Northern Heights. There were forts up there before the Conquest, and since then the defences have been extended by nervous and/or far-sighted monarchs. Inside the walls ᵻis a pharos, a lighthouse of Roman origin. Also a Saxon church, St. Mary de Castro, as well as a memorial to Louis Blériot, the first cross-Channel flyer, who landed in the castle (1909). The first cross-Channel swimmer, Captain Matthew Webb, dived off Admiralty Pier (1875). In the town, St. Edmund's Chapel (thirteenth century) is one of England's smallest churches. The Hall of Maison Dieu (also thirteenth century) is now part of the Town Hall. There are striking Georgian houses in Atholl Terrace. The Western Heights, opposite the castle, are honeycombed with excavations and defensive corridors from the manic days when Bonaparte's *Grande Armée* was drilling in Boulogne. (Dover had been sacked by the French in 1295.) Now there is a borstal on the Heights.

Dover Castle

Some places to visit

A selection of houses, gardens, churches open to the public
and within eight kilometres of the Way. Most are open in
summer only; check days and times in advance.

Loseley House is seen from the Way, just west of Guildford.
It is one of Surrey's finest Elizabethan residences, featuring
the panelling from Henry VIII's Nonsuch Palace. Some of the
stone was quarried from Waverley Abbey when it was
dissolved by the same monarch. Tel. Guildford 71881/2.

Clandon Park. National Trust property, outside West Clandon, north of Newlands Corner. Built in the Palladian style,
it houses fine furniture, pictures and porcelain, in particular
Chinese porcelain birds. Tel. Guildford 222482.

Polesden Lacey (National Trust). Regency villa transformed
into a fine Edwardian house. Drawing room and library in
excellent taste. Furniture, porcelain, silver and paintings,
and lovely grounds. Tel. Bookham 52048.

Quebec House, Westerham (National Trust). Seventeenth-
century home of General Wolfe, with relics of the Canadian
campaigns. Tel. Westerham 62206.

Chartwell, south of Westerham, Churchill's country home.
His house, garden, studio, paintings and 32 hectares of park
were donated to the National Trust in 1946. Rooms furnished
much as if he still lived there. Very popular. Tel. Crockham
Hill 368.

Emmetts Garden (National Trust) on the Sevenoaks side of
Chartwell. Two hectares of hillside garden, rare trees and
shrubs, particularly fine in spring and autumn.

Leeds Castle where Catherine of Aragon lived; the grounds
are said to have been laid out by Capability Brown. Its
romantic position on the lake dates from the twelfth century.
Tel. Maidstone 65400.

Barfreston church; flint and caen stone; one of the best
Norman buildings in Kent.

How to do it

Getting there

Rail

The North Downs are pierced by railways in several places. In the south, they start from Portsmouth, Brighton, Eastbourne and Hastings, and in the north from London stations — Victoria, Waterloo, Charing Cross, Holborn Viaduct, Blackfriars, Cannon Street and London Bridge. The Guildford to Tonbridge line follows much of our path across Surrey into Kent, while the Victoria to north-east Kent coast hugs the Way from Otford to Canterbury.

Obtain a timetable from your local station, or telephone, especially on Sundays, when services are fewer and sometimes affected by engineering works. Train telephone inquiry numbers:

London 01-928 5100, *Farnham and Guildford* Woking 65251, *West Malling* Maidstone 842842, *Canterbury* 65151, *Hastings* 429325, *Brighton* 25476.

Bus

Reliable links between the major towns, but a hotch-potch of services when off the beaten track. There is, at one time or another, a bus link along nearly every moderately used road near to or crossing the Way. Very sparse services on Sundays. The following bus company telephone numbers are for checking (from west to east):

Alder Valley Guildford 75226 (not Sundays) for Farnham and Guildford

Tillingbourne Bus Co Cranleigh 6880 for Guildford, Newlands Corner and Shere (connections to the Ewhurst Green youth hostel)

Tony McCann Coaches Forest Green 218 for Guildford, Chilworth, Shere (connections to Holmbury St. Mary youth hostel)

London Country and *Green Line* from Dorking to Sevenoaks (weekdays) Reigate 42411; (Sundays) Guildford 72137, Dorking 882281, Reigate 47022, Godstone 842234, Dunton Green 315, Sevenoaks 53596

Thames Weald West Kingsdown 2244, Sevenoaks-Otford-Dartford

Maidstone and District and *East Kent* from Wrotham to Canterbury and the sea. Borough Green 882128, Medway 405251/4, Maidstone 52211, Ashford 20342, Canterbury 63482, Folkestone 53118, Dover 206813

Car parks

Some of the main areas are mentioned, but not town parking:

Surrey
St. Martha's Hill – on the west side near Tyting Farm, on the east just off Guildford Lane
Newlands Corner
West Hanger near Hollister Farm
Ranmore Common between Lillies Copse and the Trackway, and next to the Common
Box Hill a public car park opposite the Burford Hotel, and another near the view point
Reigate Hill one near drinking fountain; the other across the A217 from the tea kiosk
South Hawke near air shaft
Titsey off trackway above High Trees

Kent
Trosley Country Park (turn off beyond Vigo Inn)
Holly Hill (overlooking Snodland)
Blue Bell Hill picnic site
Hollingbourne station a kilometre from the Way, but the village streets are too narrow for parking
Devil's Kneading Trough limited laybys
Farthing Common off B2068 beyond Stowting
Valiant Sailor pub, some parking alongside the A20 from Folkestone
Chilham to avoid parking in the village square there is a car park near the fire station at the bottom of the hill

Staying there

Bed and breakfast see Ramblers' Association annual guide, obtainable from The Ramblers' Association, 1-5 Wandsworth Road, London SW8 2LJ (tel. 01-582 6878), and the English Tourist Board's *Where to Stay in South East England.*

Youth hostels are listed in the YHA handbook, obtainable from Youth Hostels Association, Trevelyan House, 8 St. Stephen's Hill, St. Albans, Hertfordshire AL1 2DY. The eight hostels on or near to the Way are (from west to east, with accommodation in brackets):
Ewhurst Green, Cranleigh, tel. Cranleigh 5334 (32); camping
Holmbury St. Mary Radnor Lane, Holmbury St. Mary, Dorking, tel. Dorking 730777 (56); camping
Tanners Hatch Polesden Lacey, Dorking, tel. Bookham 52528 (40); camping
Crockham Hill Edenbridge, tel. Crockham Hill 322 (47)

Kemsing Cleves, Pilgrims' Way, Kemsing, Sevenoaks, tel.
Sevenoaks 61341 (64); camping
Canterbury 54 New Dover Road, tel. Canterbury 62911 (56)
Dover Town Hillesden House, 14 Godwyne Road, tel. Dover
201698 (66)
Dover Central Charlton House, 306 London Road, tel. Dover
201314 (69)

Camp sites (from west) need to be booked beforehand
Surrey
South of Tilford village (4 km from Farnham), Waverley DC
Leisure and Cultural Services Department, tel. Godalming
4104
High Ashurst 2 km north of Box Hill village; The Warden,
tel. Leatherhead 77239
Pilgrim Fort camp at Fosterdown Fort, Croydon Education
Department, tel. 01-686 4433 ext. 2258
Kent
No official camp sites in Kent as yet

General information

**General information on accommodation, transport, places
of interest, contact:**
South East England Tourist Board, Cheviot House, 4-6
Monson Road, Tunbridge Wells, Kent TN1 1NH (tel. 40766),
or locally:
Farnham Locality Office, South Street, tel. Godalming 4104
Guildford Civic Hall, London Road, tel. Guildford 67314
Rochester Eastgate Cottage, Eastgate, High Street, tel.
Medway 43666
Maidstone The Gate House, Old Palace Gardens, tel. Maid-
stone 671361
Canterbury 22 St. Peter's Street, tel. Canterbury 66567
Folkestone Harbour Street, tel. Folkestone 58594; and (May
to Sept) Pedestrian Precinct, Sandgate Road, tel. Folkestone
53840
Dover Townwall Street, tel. Dover 205108; Town Hall, tel.
Dover 206941; and (summer only) Portakabin, A2 Diversion,
Whitfield, tel. Dover 820650

Other useful addresses:
London Tourist Board, 26 Grosvenor Gardens, London
SW1W 0DU tel. 01-730 0791
English Tourist Board, 4 Grosvenor Gardens, London SW1W
0DU tel. 01-730 3400

Book list

Two books in particular have provided material and/or stimulated my thinking. The first, *Kent — the Garden of England,* by Paul Burnham and Stuart McRae (Paul Norbury, 1978), is as good an intelligent person's guide to a county as I have seen. The second, *The Theft of the Countryside* by Marion Shoard (Temple Smith, 1980), is a six-gun shoot-out at those who would despoil the English countryside. Other books include:

Chalkways of South and South-East England Edward C. Pyatt (David and Charles)
The Pilgrims' Way Seán Jennett (Cassell, 1971)
The Buildings of England ed. Nikolaus Pevsner — *Surrey; West Kent and the Weald;* and *North East and East Kent* (Penguin)
Understanding English Place-Names William Addison (Futura, 1978)
The Oxford Literary Guide to the British Isles ed. Dorothy Eagle and Hilary Carnell (OUP, 1977)
Rural Rides William Cobbett, *The Canterbury Tales* Geoffrey Chaucer, and *A tour through the whole island of Great Britain* Daniel Defoe (all available in Penguin)
The Wild Flowers of Britain and Northern Europe Richard and Alastair Fitter (Collins, 1974)
A Field Guide to the Trees of Britain and Northern Europe Alan Mitchell (Collins, 1974)
The Birds of Britain and Europe Heinzel, R. Fitter and Parslow (Collins, 1972)
The Observer's Book of Wild Flowers Francis Rose, and of *Butterflies* W. J. Stokoe (Warne)
Natural History in the Rochester Area ed. I. K. Champion and E. E. Floodgate (Rochester and District Natural History Society, 1977)
The Sunday Times Book of the Countryside Clarke, Jackman, Mercer, Crook (Macdonald, 1980)
The Domesday Geography of South-East England ed. H. C. Darby and E. M. J. Campbell (Cambridge University Press, 1962)
Portrait of Surrey Basil Cracknell (Hale, 1970).

The Country Code

Enjoy the countryside and respect its life and work

Guard against all risk of fire

Fasten all gates

Keep your dogs under close control

Keep to public paths across farmland

Use gates and stiles to cross fences, hedges and walls

Leave livestock, crops and machinery alone

Take your litter home

Help to keep all water clean

Protect wildlife, plants and trees

Take special care on country roads

Make no unnecessary noise

Norman church
Patrixbourne

146